The ABC's of College Life

The ABC's of College Life

Vicki Salemi

Writers Club Press
San Jose New York Lincoln Shanghai

The ABC's of College Life

Writers Club Press
an imprint of iUniverse, Inc.

For information address:
iUniverse, Inc.
5220 S. 16th St., Suite 200
Lincoln, NE 68512
www.iuniverse.com

ISBN: 0-595-20590-9

Printed in the United States of America

Dedication

For Debbie, my sister and best friend. You truly are the wind beneath my wings.

Epigraph

"In her down-to-earth, "you only go to college once, so don't blow it" friendly style, author Vicki Salemi earns an A+ with her debut guide for teens, *The ABC's of College Life*. No college concept is lost amongst this innovatively humorous, yet resourceful guide. From "dean's excuse" and "frisbee" to "dust balls" and "funky food"—Salemi's entries make the grade when it comes to conveying a real-life portrayal of those hallowed (and hysterical) halls of higher ed."

Gina LaGuardia
Editor-in-Chief, The CollegeBound Network

CONTENTS

FOREWORD

"These are days you'll remember. Never before and never since, I promise, will the whole world be as warm as this. And as you feel it, you'll know it's true that you are blessed and lucky. It's true that you are touched by something that will grow and bloom in you."

"These Are Days"
Lyrics by Natalie Merchant

Acknowledgements

At this point I need to thank some special people, without whom this book would not have been possible. Thanks to...

My parents for your love, support and for paying my tuition.

Lafayette College for an excellent education. The outstanding professors, beautiful campus, family-like environment and endless opportunities make it a spectacular place to live and learn.

My friends and classmates from Lafayette, especially the sisters of Alpha Gamma Delta, for the special memories on College Hill.

Everyone and everything that made my Lafayette education an awesome experience such as Dr. Campenni's Psych 101 class, 3rd Floor Easton Girls, All College Day, cocktails, pre-parties and spinning! This inspired me to create a dictionary of private jokes and Lafayette lingo which later evolved into the concept of this book.

Introduction

So you've taken all the tests, done lots of activities and finally, after searching through the catalogs and taking lots of tours, you're going to be a college freshman. There's a world of difference between high school and college: the ultimate experience in which the most important lessons learned don't always come from the classroom.

This street-smart guide spills the beans on everything from cafeteria food to co-ed dorms, from midterms to mixers, from professors to power naps. Traditions, tales and pranks at countless schools are also dished out with a heaping portion of the inside scoop of college life. Finally, the inside scoop wouldn't be complete without a categorized workbook to document your own experiences such as your worst laundry mishap.

The ABC's tell it like it is, preparing you for the journey of a lifetime. Whether you're a freshman with first-year jitters, a sophomore, junior or a super senior, you need to relearn your ABC's for the best college experience ever!

A

academics ~ the pursuit of higher education. Now that you're living away from home, hanging with friends and having an active social life, you might forget the main reason you're in college is to earn a degree.

acquaintances ~ you'll meet tons of people and never ever use their last names. You'll recognize them from your dorm, classes and parties. Typically you'll say, "Hey, what's up?" and then move on.

activities ~ there's something for everyone: school newspaper, intramural sports, rugby, crew, yearbook, student government. You name it and your school probably has it.

activities fair ~ officers and members represent their clubs at this fair during the first month of school. You can sign up and ask the officers specific questions like what the time commitments are for each club.

admissions ~ once your admitted, it's easy to forget this building exists unless you become a tour guide showing your school to prospective students.

advanced placement (AP) ~ those credits you earned in high school can actually pay off in a big way. You may be able to skip a course in the subject you aced on the AP exam.

advisor ~ similar to your guidance counselor in high school, this professor will help determine your courseload.

after hours/late-night ~ something that occurs after midnight, usually after the library closes or when the party shuts down. Example: "I'll take a study break after hours and meet you at the coffee house."

air conditioning ~ yeah, you wish. The dorms are small, it gets hot and you'll soon discover the fans you brought don't make it any cooler. Go to the air-conditioned library to cool off instead.

alarm clock ~ you hated it in high school, you'll hate it now. Waking up now isn't any easier, especially when you're hitting the books 'til the wee hours of the morning.

all-night study room ~ this room in the library is open 24 hours a day, 7 days a week. Frightening as it may seem, you might actually end up here.

all-nighter ~ it's 10 p.m., you have 10 hours of studying to do and the exam is at 8 a.m. You do the math.

alma mater ~ song usually composed by an alum like 100 years ago in honor of your school. Also, to alumni this is their school.

Animal House ~ movie that depicts old-time college and fraternity life as a huge wild 'n crazy beer guzzling toga party.

apartments ~ alternative to living in the dorms, this is typically the housing preference for upperclassmen.

athletics ~ whether you're an athlete yourself or a school-spirited fan, there's nothing quite like college sports—football, basketball, lacrosse, field hockey, you name it.

attendance ~ as in actually going to class. Professors may do roll call in small classes so you can boost that grade simply by showing up.

automatic 4.0 ~ rumor has it your GPA will automatically be a 4.0 if your roommate dies even though this has yet to be confirmed in any university handbook. That's one morbid way to earn straight A's!

automatic teller machines (ATM) ~ your prime money source for cash on demand. Though it's convenient to have cash at your fingertips, it could be fatal to your bank account.

B

BA ~ a Bachelor of Arts degree.

baccalaureate ~ a farewell address to graduates.

bachelor's degree or a bachelor's ~ an undergrad degree such as the BA, BS or BBA.

backpacks ~ wear one and you too can look like Joe College. Everyone uses these for class, the library, the gym and yes, the cafeteria (take home food for later!).

bagels 'n beer ~ a party in the morning. Synonymous with **eggs 'n kegs**.

bands ~ get some friends together and perform on campus or join the marching band to bolster school spirit! Your school may have lots of other bands, like a jazz band or classical orchestra so be sure to check them out!

bathrooms ~ are gross. When you go home you will appreciate the little things in life like a clean sink, a shower with lighting and some privacy.

battle of the bands ~ annual campus event when lots of student bands play and compete for the title of best band. Great opportunity to relax with friends and catch some good tunes.

BBA ~ a bachelor's degree in Business Administration.

bedtime ~ anything goes! Some nights you'll finish studying at midnight, other times it'll be 2 a.m. and sometimes you may not go to sleep at all. See **all-nighter**.

beer goggles ~ for those of legal drinking age, this is impaired vision and judgment as a result of alcohol which makes an unattractive person look a whole lot better.

bicycles ~ one mode of transportation to class, especially useful at a large campus.

bid ~ an invitation to join a sorority or fraternity that officially marks the end of rushing and the beginning of Greek life.

bid day ~ the day people get their bids. So you've made it this far, you haven't dropped out of rush, you stuck with it and now you're waiting for the biggest day of all. Hopefully you'll get a bid from the house you really, really like. If so, you'll meet everyone in your pledge class and go to the house to hang out and celebrate with your future brothers/sisters. If not, don't worry. You can always rush again next year.

big brother/big sister ~ older person in your fraternity or sorority who's supposed to be like your big brother or big sis and look out for you. Think of this as a little family within a bigger family (your fraternity or sorority).

birthdays ~ great reason to party! (But who needs a reason?)

bizarre buildings ~ most buildings are named after the person who donated the big bucks to build it.

blood drives ~ besides the fact that it's a great cause, usually there's lots of free food.

"blow off" class ~ easy course you can sleep through and still ace, such as the Anthropology of Sports. Note: sometimes a blow off class will get a facelift and suddenly become very difficult. To avoid struggling through "Rocks for Jocks", ask upperclassmen which classes are really blow offs.

blue book ~ light blue pamphlet with 8 pages which may be used to answer essay questions on exams.

BMOC ~ big man on campus.

bonding ~ situation that brings people closer together such as pledges who spend an entire weekend at the house rehearsing their song for the annual lip sync contest.

books ~ you'll spend a few hundred bucks on these each semester.

bookstore ~ home of the official college sweatshirt. It's the place to purchase your books, school supplies and miscellaneous stuff like gum and magazines. Consider it one-stop shopping for your family's holiday presents, as well as the place to stock up on t-shirts, sweatshirts, coffee mugs and school paraphernalia.

bouncer ~ big guy who stands in the entrance of a bar in order to card people. His job is to scrutinize IDs and ensure underage drinkers do not enter the bar.

brainstorms ~ occur when you least expect it. Don't be surprised if you wake up in the middle of the night and finally pick a topic for your sociology paper.

break ~ fall break, winter break, spring break, stop me anytime now…

breakfast ~ still the most important meal of the day, even though college students don't wake up until noon on weekends. It's also the best meal you'll eat in the cafeteria. After all, how could they mess up toast? Note: meals get worse as the day progresses. Lunch is OK but dinner really stinks. See **cereal**.

brothers ~ members of a fraternity.

BS ~ a load of bull#@!?. Just kidding. Also stands for a Bachelor of Science degree.

bucket ~ use this as a container to hold your toiletries in the bathroom.

bulletin boards ~ you'll wish you had one of these when it's two weeks into the semester and you have no idea where you put your course schedule.

bumper sticker ~ your parents will buy this sticker for their cars that states: "My money and my kid go to __________ University." (insert your school's name here)

bunkbeds ~ essential in smaller dorm rooms. It's not so easy to climb into one, but it's very easy to fall out. Beware!

bursar ~ the school's official treasurer.

BYOB ~ "bring your own beer" parties where everyone can attend but those of legal drinking age supply beverages for their consumption only. Of course, you've got the less popular BYOB party where people actually bring their own fruit. That's right, it stands for "Bring Your Own Banana".

C

caf ~ the mess hall. If you try hard enough and zone out the food, it's a great way to socialize and spend time with friends.

cafeteria food ~ ever heard of mystery meat? Your worst nightmares have come true! Don't let the tour guide fool you. It really is bad.

cafeteria trays ~ forget its primary use in the caf. These trays are great make-shift sleds! Expect to see a shortage of trays after the first snow-storm when everyone on campus goes sledding down the biggest hill on campus. Wheeeeee!

caffeine ~ a mandatory substance when pulling all-nighters.

camp ~ it will feel like you're in one. Besides being away from home and attending classes, the rest of your schedule is flexible and you're surrounded by people your own age. You can do whatever you want or as college kids say, you get to *play*.

campus ~ all the buildings at your school and the challenge of figuring out where everything is!

campus crawl ~ for those of legal drinking age this is the act of going from one party to the next, drinking a beer at each place.

campus events ~ stay on campus and check out all the events like academic lectures, comedians, and musical events.

campus intranet ~ go online and gain access to bulletin boards, course info and if you're lucky, some campus chat rooms.

campus mail ~ consider this inter-office mail in campus terms. Mostly at small schools, you don't need to put a stamp on mail that is sent to someone on campus.

campus phones ~ phones placed throughout campus and outside locked dorms, especially convenient when you accidentally leave your key in your room and need your roommate to let you back inside.

carding ~ act of showing the bouncer your ID in order to enter a bar. Note: if you're underage, the bouncer will easily spot your fake ID as an imposter. Why else would it be called fake?

careers ~ what your parents think you're preparing for while you're in college. Choosing a career can be totally overwhelming considering it's hard enough declaring a major!

career center ~ go there to avoid a huge line after graduation (that is, the unemployment one!). The folks here can help you pick a major, find an internship, keep you on the job track and remind you that life exists beyond the ivy covered buildings.

cars ~ not a big deal if you don't have one but it gives you a little more freedom if you do. Most schools require students to get parking permits. On most campuses freshmen are not encouraged to have cars because parking spaces are in short supply.

cereal ~ still hungry after eating that bowl of chili pea soup? Not satisfied with the serving of beef goulash? Instead of having cereal at breakfast, try some at dinner! Cheerios, Lucky Charms and Fruit Loops are the standards of any cereal selection. The caf should have cereal available all day long, something to keep in mind when your main entrée is both unidentifiable and unappetizing.

chancellor ~ at some schools this is the same thing as the president. At other schools it's simply a high level official.

chapter ~ a local branch of a fraternity or sorority. Although a national fraternity or sorority will exist at many schools, each chapter may be different. Translation: members of one chapter may be nerds while members of the same organization at another school may be total jocks.

cheating ~ quick way to get expelled from school, lose the semester's tuition or get a zero on the exam. Schools have their own honor codes with policies on issues such as cheating or plagiarizing.

chocolate chip cookies ~ the one yummy thing worth eating in the cafeteria these days.

chug ~ to take a drink in one big gulp. Dozing off in front of your computer at 4 a.m., your psych paper's due in a few hours and you're still struggling with the introduction. Need a quick fix of caffeine? Time to chug some Mountain Dew, fast!! (Of course, the common beer chug comes to mind too!)

class is canceled! Yay! When professors don't live near campus, bad weather means they may not make it to class. Since you're not in high school anymore, a whole day of classes won't be canceled. Instead, the only class cancellations will be the ones your professors miss. Translation: despite the bad weather some profs may make it to campus after all.

class is outside! If class isn't canceled, this is the next best thing. Inspired by the arrival of sunny spring days, ask the prof if you can have class outside. If they're up for it, you'll all go outside and catch some rays while the prof teaches.

class nicknames ~ if you think only people have nicknames in college, think again. Actual classes have nicknames too. Check this out:

Rocks for Jocks—Geology 101
Nuts and Sluts—Abnormal Psychology
Clapping for Credit—Music 101
Shake and Bake—Earthquakes and Volcanoes
Spots and Dots—Modern Art
Baby Chem—Chemistry 101
Cell Hell—Cellular Molecular Biology
Blabs in Labs—Linguistics

class rings ~ don't even think about wearing your high school ring! (It'll look like you're still into the high school scene.)

class size ~ varies. Some of your classes will have only ten students and others may have as many as a thousand depending on the size of your school and the course. Intro courses usually are larger while upper level classes have fewer students.

closet space ~ is tiny. This is a given. Pack as much as you can into it and then create more space by using underbed storage bins and crates.

co-ed bathrooms ~ if you live on a co-ed floor, bathrooms may be shared between males AND females! If you live on a single-sex floor there's no need to worry.

co-ed floors ~ guys and girls are next door neighbors. These living conditions aren't as crazy as they seem. Hallmates may form close bonds like brothers and sisters.

coffee ~ one of the four food groups for college students. You know them, right? Pizza, cereal, coffee and more pizza.

college ~ four years of higher education that you'll have for the rest of your life. Open books and you will open your mind! You'll live in a dorm and go out every night of the week, whether it's for an academic lecture, basketball game or comedian on campus. Try out for the drama club, take a philosophy course, learn how to paint in watercolors, form an alternative rock band. Live it! Love it!

commencement ~ fancy word for graduation.

committees ~ itty bitty way of breaking down a big task in an organization to get things done. For example, organizing a teeter-totter-a-thon would involve a committee for publicity, fundraising and scheduling everyone's turn on the teeter-totter.

community service ~ be a good do-be and volunteer for programs like soup kitchens and adopt-a-grandparent.

commuter students ~ students who don't live on campus have the tedious task of finding a parking space day after day.

composite ~ poster that has lots of tiny pictures of everyone in the sorority or fraternity. Most houses have a huge framed composite in their entrance hallway. Note: some houses bolt this big composite to the wall so a rival house can't steal it!

computer games ~ beware of solitaire. See **procrastination.**

contact lenses ~ if you wear them, plan to lose at least one. When you come home at 3 a.m. on homecoming weekend and toss your keys on a pile of dirty clothes, take out your contacts in the dark and put them on your dresser with all the drawers open, it would be a miracle to find both contact lenses in the morning.

convocation ~ the official welcome into college, usually consisting of the President or Dean's speech, "Look to your right, look to your left, these people will be your best friends for the rest of your life."

course catalog ~ annual book or online catalog that lists course titles, descriptions, credits and professors. A new catalog should be available each fall and spring so be sure to read most updated edition when choosing your classes or else you'll inadvertently register for a course that is not offered.

course schedule ~ list that tells you the day, time and location of each class you signed up for. You'll get this schedule at the beginning of each semester.

courses ~ you'll probably have four or five courses each semester. If you want a lighter courseload one semester you'll have to balance it out with a heavier load later on.

cramming ~ last minute ugly act of studying a ton of information in a ridiculously small amount of time, usually involving a lot of caffeine, a lot of stress and little or no sleep.

crash ~ you weren't invited to a party but you really want to go. So you show up and crash it. Also, let's say you pull an all-nighter and for a brief moment you feel wide awake. You are totally wired and then suddenly, out of nowhere, it hits you big time and you're completely exhausted.

crates ~ great way to maximize and organize that dorm space. Each square plastic container costs only a few bucks and can store absolutely anything such as clothes, books and food.

credit card ~ watch out! Plastic could easily be your worst enemy. Whether you're buying books or charging airfare for spring break, those bills add up and late fees are not cheap.

cum laude ~ the honor roll of all honor rolls. Criteria may differ at each school, but it's usually graduating with a GPA between 3.5 and 3.65.

cumulative ~ you don't want your finals to be like this. A cumulative exam includes everything you learned the entire semester which includes info that was taught on the very first day of class. Yikes!

current events ~ like you're really going to have any time to watch the news. It's easy to forget the world exists out there unless you log on to a news-related website.

curtains or blinds ~ without them your dorm windows will look a little naked.

cut throat or "a throat" ~ student who wants to be one-up on everyone else. This person is extremely secretive and uncooperative when it comes to sharing info. Major symptoms are turning assignments in early, constantly contributing to class and being in the professor's face the whole semester.

D

daily planner ~ constantly on the go, you'll need to keep track of all the important dates for exams, papers, all your activities, social events and the big home football games.

dance marathon ~ philanthropy that raises money whereby you rock around the clock for 24 hours and then collapse. (But hey, it's okay —it's for charity!)

damages ~ fees you must pay at the end of the year for things like the fire extinguisher on your hall that was stolen or the holes you made in your wall from hanging stuff.

date parties/crush parties ~ parties held by a fraternity or sorority in which the only requirement is bringing a date.

dean ~ like your high school principal, only now there's one for each function of college administration, such as Dean of Student Affairs, Dean of Greek Life and Dean of Residence Halls.

dean's excuse ~ think of this as the parent excuses you got in high school for absences. You can get a written excuse to miss class or exams if you have a legitimate reason, like attending a funeral.

dean's list ~ honor roll which is typically signified by getting a 3.5 or higher for a semester.

dice/deck of cards ~ simple necessities used for playing games when hanging out in the dorms.

dictionary ~ chances are this will sit on your shelf collecting dust. You'll be studying in the library so much that you'll end up using the library's dictionary instead of your own.

diploma ~ the spiffy piece of paper that represents those hard earned credits.

directory ~ the campus phone book of students and faculty.

discussion ~ intellectual conversation. Rack up class participation points by reading all your assignments and volunteering to talk in class. Hey, if you participate on your own you'll decrease your chances of being called on unexpectedly when you're not prepared.

dj ~ you can be one! Get your own radio show on the campus station and play the music you want to hear. You'll probably have to be an intern first, report the news for a semester or two and eventually work your way up to hosting your own show.

doctors ~ most of your professors, if not all, will have their PhDs. Instead of calling your prof Professor Allan, the proper form of address is Doctor Allan.

door duty/sitting security ~ a campus bash in which students take turns playing bouncer and check student IDs.

dorms ~ your home away from home. Though your school probably calls these residence halls, it's the one place other than the library where you think you can study. Until you try hitting the books and get distracted by things like friends, the phone and yes, the remote control. Your dorm room will soon become several rooms rolled into one: living room (watch tv, hang with friends), kitchen (microwave mac and cheese) and yes, your sleeping quarters.

double major ~ two majors (duh). At some schools you can actually graduate with a bachelor's degree in two departments, such as Economics and English.

dress code ~ there is none! Comfort is key and no one really cares if you wear your pajamas to class.

drop/add ~ time period at the start of each semester in which you can alter your schedule by dropping some classes and adding others. Great opportunity to consider dropping that 8 a.m. class you know you'll never make it to.

dry clean only ~ okay, since you'll barely do your laundry you think you'll really get something dry cleaned? Maybe you'll go there once or twice a semester to get a shirt pressed or formal dress cleaned but that's about it.

dry erase marker ~ use this to write on the message board on your door so message can be erased by a quick swipe of your hand. Note: these markers will easily get lost when other people will borrow yours to write on neighbors' doors and forget to put your marker back on your door.

drying rack ~ funky wooden structure used to dry towels, underwear and any other laundry. Extremely useful because dryers only turn wet clothes into damp clothes.

dues ~ semester or annual membership fees paid to a sorority or fraternity. Depending on the organization and whether your dues include a meal plan, fees could range from a few hundred bucks per semester to a thousand.

dust balls ~ with a full courseload, activities and an intense social life, who has time to dust?

E

education ~ you will learn as much outside the classroom as you will learn in it.

eggs 'n kegs ~ a party before noon. Also known as **bagels 'n beer**.

eight a.m. class ~ early class you'll be tempted to skip. The 8 a.m. is the kiss of death on the schedule. You'll roll out of bed, go to class, go home and climb right back into bed. (That is, as long as you don't have a 9 a.m. class immediately following it!)

elections ~ cast a ballot, you political machine. Vote on campus for your favorite candidate in student government elections or even decide to run for office yourself. As for big elections out in the real world, get an absentee ballot and mail in your vote.

electives ~ courses not in your major or minor but they totally round out your schedule and make you well-rounded. Examples are public speaking and the history of jazz.

e-mail ~ the greatest and quickest way to keep in touch with high school friends. Yet another way to procrastinate when you're sitting in front of the computer, postponing writing that philosophy paper.

empty nest ~ lonely feeling your family may experience after you move away. Your family will either experience this or they will get over it and convert your room into a home gym.

evaluations ~ like a small consolation prize after attending all those classes and doing the work, it's your turn to grade the professor. You'll get to rate your profs' abilities in different areas like teaching style and grading method. Your comments provide feedback to the administration and faculty.

exams ~ college word for tests that usually occur several times during the semester. They could be multiple choice, essay or maybe even a take home. Whatever the format is, study everything.

extra long sheets ~ because those mattresses are extra long.

F

face book ~ picture directory which includes basic information on freshmen like their names, campus addresses and their photos.

face time ~ time spent congregating in a popular place where it's likely you'll be seen and see others, such as the mailroom in the student center at lunchtime.

fall break ~ this four day break occurs over Columbus Day weekend and will most likely be the first time you'll come home since you started school. You'll hang with old friends, sleep in your own bed and eat real food. Don't bother bringing any books home because they won't even make it out of the backpack. Enjoy being home, enjoy your own bathroom and not eating food off of a cafeteria tray.

family ~ your friends will become your surrogate family. They will see you at your best, they will see you at your worst and they will love you anyway.

fatal disk error ~ you do not want this to appear on your computer screen after you've cranked out a 30 page lab report. Once you get this message, it's GAME OVER. Moral of the story: save that document on more than one disk.

field trip ~ you will be just as excited about these as you were in elementary school. It doesn't happen a lot but every once in a while a class will go on a little trip, such as a music class to a concert, an art class to a museum, you get the idea...

fifth year senior ~ someone who didn't quite finish on the four year plan.

finals ~ stressful week at the end of each semester when you take exams covering the entire content of each course. If you have five classes you'll probably have five finals. You'll live in the library, which extends its hours. Don't plan on having much of a social life 'cause parties are less happening during finals.

finals in the gym ~ if your school is huge, chances are your classes are too and you'll take finals in the gym. Bring your school ID, a pencil, pen and of course, your thinking cap. School IDs are closely monitored so don't even think of having a friend take the final for you. It doesn't work that way.

finals package ~ care package your parents send to help get you through cramming for finals. Typical contents include oreos and microwave popcorn.

finals schedule ~ your way of knowing where, when and at what time each final will be taken. You know you have a really bad schedule when you have to two finals scheduled in the same day. Even worse is having an exam scheduled on the last possible day finals are given. At that point practically everyone else has already gone home and the campus is a virtual ghost town.

financial aid ~ financial assistance with costs for a worthy cause: you!

fire drills ~ thought you left these behind? Think again. Fire drills in the dorms will go off during the middle of winter at 3 a.m., the night before your big economics exam. Some schools make their resident advisors issue monetary fines to students who remain in their room during a drill. Definitely keep the following fire safety tips in mind:

- Always find out where the nearest exit is when you're at a party, in the library, or in class.
- Don't plug an extension cord into every outlet if you use a power strip.
- If you light candles, make sure you blow them out before leaving your room. And of course make sure they're not located near curtains (that's assuming you actually have curtains!)
- If you smoke make sure your cigarette is put out in an ashtray and not a garbage can.

first-year student ~ politically correct term for a freshman.

flip flops ~ because those showers give new meaning to the words "soap scum".

folklore ~ unusual class covering topics like traditions, beliefs, legends and lore. Reading *Cinderella* may actually be an assignment! This is one of those electives you should look into.

formal event ~ an ultra chic party that requires you to get a date. Formals are usually held by sororities and fraternities each semester, though some groups such as dorms may have formals too. Girls and guys get dressed up and go somewhere like a hotel where they eat dinner, hang out, dance and have a great time!

founders day ~ day that acknowledges the person or people who founded your school.

4.0 ~ the highest GPA you can get, the definition of straight As. But the real challenge is getting a 4.0 AND having a life!

fourth floor (or fifth or sixth...) ~ like you really wanna go up and down 200 stairs about five times a day? If you want buns of steel, then live on the top floor of a dorm that doesn't have any elevators!

fouton ~ a comfy chair that opens up to a bed. Perfect for when your roommate has a guest and kicks you out. Move the fouton to a friend's room down the hall and crash there.

fraternity ~ group of guys in a Greek organization. Fraternities are clubs with secret rituals, officers and meetings. They also sponsor charitable fundraisers, throw parties and give their members an instant social life.

fraternity row ~ this is literally a row of frat houses. At some schools all the fraternity houses are located next to one another in one area of campus.

free ride ~ as in, full tuition is covered by a scholarship. No loans, no debt, no problems!

freedom ~ never before and never again will you have so much of this. In the course of one day you can take a nap, workout, visit friends and watch *General Hospital.* Your only real responsibilities are on the syllabus. Yeah!

freshman ~ like this really needs a definition?

freshman fifteen ~ pounds, that is, and you're lucky if that's all you gain! Here's a little list of pointers to keep in mind:

- Stay active. Go to the gym, go for walks, exercise. Do something to get out of your sedentary (translation: couch potato) ways. Even though you'll be busy studying, you're basically sitting in one place for a long time.
- You may be so stressed that you want something gooey and fried (don't we all need that sometimes?) but try not to make this your daily dose of stress relief. In the caf the options may be less than stellar, but you know there will always be lunch meat like turkey.
- In addition to 3 meals a day, you're bound to be snacking during the day and throughout the night. Opt for microwave popcorn or pretzels over potato chips or nachos with salsa. Have this stuff handy so you don't feel the need to get take-out Chinese food when your friends ask you to join in.
- Pizza used to be something you ate as a meal, but now it's a way to hang out with friends and take a break from solving Calc problems at midnight. It's fun at first, but like everything else you shouldn't make this a habit. Not only will you feel a hit in your bank account, you'll need to go shopping for jeans in a bigger size! Ouch!

friday afternoons ~ after a tedious week of work the most carefree afternoon doesn't come soon enough! You can tell it's time to relax when the library clears out at 3 p.m. and doesn't get crowded again until Sunday night.

friends ~ you can't exactly remember how you met them but you can't picture life without 'em.

frisbee ~ toss a frisbee! It's fun, it's free and it's on the quad on a really nice day.

froyo (frozen yogurt) ~ no wonder why it's so popular. It's either this or the vegetarian chili slop served at dinner.

FUN, FUN, FUN! ~ college is a blast. Formals, mixers, Halloween, spring break! At no other time in your life will you be surrounded by people your own age, to live, study and play with 24 hours a day, 7 days a week!

fundraisers ~ buy a t-shirt, send a carnation, all for a good cause.

funky food ~ self-explanatory. Here's a list of some not-so yummy cafeteria concoctions:

> Yamburgers—if a yam is a sweet potato and a burger is a burger, why would anyone combine the two?
> Barbecued egg meatballs—ewwwwwww!
> Stuffed grape leaves—stuffed what?
> Chicketti—what the heck is it? Note: only eat food you've heard of.
> Green Falafel burgers—a green burger? How unappetizing is that?
> Salami surprise soup—avoid any food that has the word 'surprise' in its name!

fun tac ~ blue gooey stuff used to stick posters and decorations on the wall.

G

games ~ calling all the oxen free! Consider yourself a kid at heart and go with it when the mood strikes. That's right, go ahead and play a game of Hide and Go Seek at night with your buddies. A campus is an awesome place to play this game, as you can hide behind statues, behind bushes, in doorways in buildings, in the stacks in the library...the possibilities are endless!

garbage bags ~ the suitcase alternative. These bags provide the perfect way to pack. Toss clothes into bags and then throw bags into car.

geography ~ after meeting loads of people from tons of places, you will learn about tiny towns that you never knew existed.

germs ~ the minute someone has the flu on campus, the whole health center will be full of sick students.

good stuff boxes ~ goody boxes distributed to dorms at the beginning of each year. Contents include the essentials of college life: packs of laundry detergent, gum, highlighters and aspirin.

gossip ~ you will know more information about people than you'd ever care to know. Scary thing is, they'll know just as much about you.

grad students ~ students in even higher learning may teach some of your classes and labs.

GPA (a.k.a. grade point average) ~ the number that matters most. Based on a 4.0 scale at most schools, your GPA is calculated using every grade you earn. The overall GPA is determined by all the classes you take while your major GPA is determined by courses in your major.

grades ~ you used to call this your report card.

graduation ~ these four years will fly. Each semester will flow into the next and before you know it, you're sitting at commencement pondering your future, wondering where the past four years went.

Grease ~ this movie soundtrack is more popular now than it ever was. Go Greased Lightning!

GREs, LSATs, MCATs ~ entrance exams for even higher education. No need to think about these until junior year.

The Greek Alphabet

Alpha	Α	Nu	Ν
Beta	Β	Xi	Ξ
Gamma	Γ	Omicron	Ο
Delta	Δ	Pi	Π
Epsilon	Ε	Rho	Ρ
Zeta	Ζ	Sigma	Σ
Eta	Η	Tau	Τ
Theta	θ	Upsilon	Υ
Iota	Ι	Phi	Φ
Kappa	Κ	Chi	Χ
Lambda	Λ	Psi	Ψ
Mu	Μ	Omega	Ω

Greeks ~ members of fraternities and sororities are part of Greek life so they're considered "Greek".

Greek Week ~ week long competition between fraternities and sororities, usually held in the spring. Houses participate in events like pie eating contests and tricycle races. At the end of the week awards are granted for the events and honors are bestowed such as the house with the highest GPA.

greeting cards ~ cheap and convenient substitute for presents. Since you won't have time to buy gifts for your pals and you certainly won't have the money, send cards instead.

group projects ~ assignment for 3 or 4 people in your class to do together. Immediately divide the project into tasks so one or two people don't end up doing all the work.

group studying ~ get a group of 4 or 5 people and reserve a soundproof room in the library get together in someone's dorm for a few hours. You can share knowledge, share notes and if you're having fun, maybe even share a pizza.

guitar ~ yes, some people play this in their dorm room. No, not all of them are talented.

gum chewing ~ finally you're at a place where professors really don't care if you chew gum in class. Most don't care if you eat in class either, just as long as you don't disturb everyone. Think of the sound a bag of pretzels makes when opened. Open the bag before you get to class to avoid the stares from glaring classmates, not to mention the jealousy if they're hungry!

gym ~ great place to burn off steam and calories and most of all, hang out with friends. Usually opens early and closes late which is great for our long days full of classes, studying and socializing.

H

Halloween ~ a huge party night plus a great excuse to wear a costume and act silly. In high school you didn't dare think about dressing up but now you can't imagine not.

hall pass ~ yeah, right! There's no need for passes any more. After all, you're in college and it's certainly not high school. If you need to leave, just get up and quietly exit the classroom.

halogen lamp ~ this lamp has been known to start fires. Stay away from clip on lamps, too (another fire hazard). For all you candle lovers out there, always blow out those candles in your room before you go to sleep or leave your room (as if you didn't already know).

hangovers ~ punishment to all the 21-year olds for drinking too much. You'll feel as if you got run over by a Mack truck which makes you wonder if the partying was really worth it?

hazing ~ secretive acts pledges must endure in order to get initiated into their fraternity or sorority. The official line is that hazing no longer exists, but it's just gone undercover. Pledges don't talk about hazing so no one outside the organization really knows what's going on.

"heads up!" ~ a strange phenomenon of dorm bathrooms increases the temperature of shower water when a toilet is flushed. To avoid this shock, as a courtesy yell "heads up" before you flush. This tells the person in the shower to jump away from the faucet because in a second when the toilet is flushed the water will immediately become scalding hot. Yikes!

health center ~ the campus doctor's office. It's usually included in the cost of tuition so you might as well use it even if it's only to get free aspirin.

healthy ~ don't plan to be. You'll live on coffee and pizza. You call that healthy?

hectic ~ as in, your life will be. But it's a good kind of hectic by balancing classes, a social life, sports, activities and some good old-fashioned hanging out with friends. You'll love it.

hell week ~ the last week of pledging in a fraternity, right before initiation, usually consisting of intense hazing.

highlighters ~ a rainbow assortment of note taking pleasures.

high school ~ is a thing of the past. It doesn't matter if you were president of your class or a varsity athlete. You're in college and it's time to begin a new chapter of your life.

homecoming ~ social event involving tailgating and a home football game. Just as you're getting used to this whole college thing, graduates return to reminisce about the good ole days.

homemade haircuts ~ save some bucks by having your roommate or friend trim your hair. Who cares if your bangs are a little crooked? It's free!

homesick ~ don't worry, you won't be. Okay, at first you might miss your friends, your family and your old way of life. It's almost healthy to be homesick so don't freak out if you're a little unhappy at first. There's no real trick to cure homesickness so keep that chin up and eventually things just fall into place. Then when you go home for break you'll be homesick for your new home: your school!

hometowns ~ if you have a girlfriend/boyfriend at home, this is what she/he is called. "I can't go with you to the formal because I have a hometown," is something you'll rarely hear. You won't know who has a hometown and who doesn't, mainly because a lot of people aren't faithful to their long-distance loves.

homework ~ endless stream of reading assignments, labs, research, papers, presentations, exams and quizzes that will make your senior year of high school seem like a breeze.

honor societies ~ exist for about every major and look great on a resume. Your advisor or professor may need to nominate you or you may have to fill out an application. Find out about these in your junior year.

hook-up ~ means anything from an innocent kiss to "shacking up" and includes everything in between.

hot pot ~ portable cooking gadget you need to make mac and cheese.

house ~ sorority or fraternity house where members live, hold meetings and hang out. A fraternity brother might say, "I'm going to the House to work on my Chem Lab." Also, the house represents all the members in your organization such as "My house wants to get tickets to a Yankees game."

housing lottery ~ although housing lotteries differ from school to school the concept is basically the same. The better the room pick, the better the chances are of getting a room you want to live in. Even if you and your future roomie have the ideal room selected for next year, a key factor is getting a good number in the housing lottery. If you choose a bad number and all the good rooms get taken first, you may end up living in a place far, far away.

I

ID ~ the really bad picture of yourself you'll get freshman year that will be used for everything from taking out library books to attending football games to eating in the caf on your meal plan.

index cards ~ these babies provide an organized, methodical way to study such as learning the background of paintings for Art History.

initiation ~ a fraternity or sorority ceremony that marks the end of pledging and the official entry into the brotherhood or sisterhood. The new members are eligible to attend meetings, run for office and even learn the secret handshake.

insurance ~ get some. If you don't have it and you get mono during midterms and have to go home, your tuition for the entire semester is down the drain.

inter-fraternity council (IFC) ~ the governing body of fraternities. IFC consists of at least one member from each fraternity on campus.

internships ~ an excellent way to earn credit and get real world experience at the same time. Usually taken instead of a class, you'll work a few hours a week and get hands-on learning. Cool internships may be at a local newspaper, radio station or politician's office to name a few. To find out more, march into your career center on campus. Although you probably won't get a paycheck for being an intern, you can gain valuable skills and contacts through the experience.

interview suit ~ the navy or black uniform all seniors wear the day of the job fair and for big on-campus interviews. Find out more about these important days by visiting the career center.

intramurals (IMs) ~ fun way to play a sport without the pressure and demanding schedule of varsity sports. Teams from social living groups such as dorms who play against each other in sports like basketball, rugby, badminton, bowling, tennis, hockey and soccer.

intro courses ~ the basic class you must take before you can take any advanced classes such as English 101, French 101, Bio 101. Most of your freshman year will be made up of intro courses.

invite-only ~ exclusive party that requires an invitation to get in.

iron ~ are you really going to use this? There are some things you have to think twice about before bringing to college. This is one of them.

J

January break ~ the holiday break after the first semester and before the second in which you can relax, hang out with high school friends and catch up on sleep you missed during those December finals.

jobs ~ there are lots of creative ways to earn money on campus. Tutor, do people's laundry, referee a volleyball game. Think of it, do it and make the cash.

Joe College ~ in his school sweatshirt, rugged baseball cap, jeans, sneaks and backpack, this typical college kid is ready for action. He's at every party, every sporting event and still manages to ace those exams.

junior year ~ crunch time. You may start research on a thesis, line up that summer internship, and take higher level courses within your major.

K

karaoke ~ at a formal, at a party or in hanging in your dorm, it's the act of singing completely off-key to songs like *Copa Cabana* and pretending you know all the words. For the first time in print, here are the all-time best karaoke tunes compiled by yours truly. For best results, sing them at the top of your lungs!

I Will Survive by Gloria Gaynor
The Gambler by Kenny Rogers
Love Shack by the B-52s
Summer Nights on the Grease Soundtrack
Respect by Aretha Franklin

keychains ~ coily spring bracelet worn on the wrist (think telephone cord) or thick string worn around the neck with a keyring attached. By wearing your keys, there's less of a chance of losing 'em.

keys ~ you'll own two very important keys: one to your dorm and the other to your mailbox. Never ever attach your keys to your ID. If you lose one, you'll automatically lose the other.

kid ~ you'll still feel like one. Let's face it, you'll nap a lot, you'll still dress up for Halloween and after four years of college you'll still be deciding what you want to be when you grow up.

kinetics ~ what exactly is this? Find out what a course is before you actually register for it.

kitchen ~ in most dorms it's located near the basement lounge and laundry room. The stove is from the 1970s and the cabinets are just as old. Don't even think about using the crusty utensils or dishes. Besides, the only time you'll cook is when you make popcorn and you can use your neighbor's microwave for that.

L

lab ~ hands-on course which meets approximately three to four hours a week. Lab courses are usually four credits and more involved than a typical class. You attend class and lab so you'll have class assignments and separate lab experiments. Not-so-favorites include bio lab (wait 'til you see what you will dissect!) and rat lab training (you too can manipulate a small animal to press a bar and get water).

ladder ~ a necessity for climbing in and out of lofts.

lamps ~ bring some. The average dorm room will have one dim ceiling light.

language lab ~ place where you will spend at least 4 hours a week, wearing big clunky earphones, listening and repeating statements such as "voy a la biblioteca con Juan" and feeling like a complete dork.

lap desk ~ ever tried doing work on your bed without having a flat surface to write on? Pretty hard, huh? Get this desk which has a pillow part for your lap and a board on top.

lap top ~ convenient for working on a paper on the quad so you can take in the fresh air and still do your work.

late ~ gone are the days when you go out and come home by midnight. Now you're lucky if you actually leave by midnight. Be prepared to go out late and come home early. Keep in mind without a curfew you won't have the 'rents to deal with but you'll be tired and may regret it for days.

laundry ~ don't mix light stuff with dark or you'll end up with pink!

Here are some tips to help you with doing the wash.

- Make sure all your jeans pockets are empty. Turn your jeans inside out if you don't want them to fade as quickly. Be sure to close all zippers, snaps and hooks on everything.
- Read those labels! Dry clean only means you'll have to go to a dry cleaner and 100% cotton means your clothes will shrink in the dryer. (Trust me, they will shrink!)
- Separate your light stuff from your dark and your delicates (that would be your underwear) from heavy ones.
- Keep other stuff all by itself, like towels and your robe. You should wash that stuff separate from your clothing.
- Choose a washing machine that's empty. This one seems pretty simple but sometimes you may find a random sock in the machine left accidentally from the person before you. Next, throw everything in it, toss in some detergent, and choose the temperature and cycle settings on the washing machine. Here's a hint: hot=whites and very very dirty clothes. Cold=darks and colors that run. Use warm water for everything else.

WARNING

Keep a close eye on your wash. If someone wants to use the machine after your finished and you are not there to remove your clothes, don't be surprised to find your clean underwear and clothes thrown around the laundry room.

Also, watch out for your generic school sweatshirt or T-shirts. While you're in the lounge watching TV, someone might be stealing your clothes.

laundry bag ~ nifty sack used to transport dirty clothes to/from laundry room. Also used to carry your laundry back home on breaks. See **visits home**.

laundry room ~ room that's usually in the basement of each dorm. If you can't find it, simply follow that fresh, fluffy scent.

lavaliere ~ a pre-pinning kind of thing, in which a guy gives his girlfriend a charm with his fraternity letters on it. This means the couple is kind of serious.

lecture ~ when your professor talks for the entire class time. Instead of dozing off, take lots and lots of notes because it's all going to be on the exam.

legacy ~ if a grandparent, parent or sibling was a member of a fraternity or sorority, you are now a legacy of that organization. Being a legacy could be helpful in getting a foot in the door if that's where you want to join.

letters ~ Greek letter clothing. "I want to wear my letters [my sorority sweatshirt], but they're in the wash."

liberal arts ~ a plethora of learning including arts and sciences. Philosophy, history and the languages are some examples.

library (a.k.a. "the libes") ~ this academic setting may be more social than the student center! On Sunday nights, the libes is the place to be. Everyone realizes it's time to hit the books and this means only one thing: the library is packed with your friends, acquaintances and people you've never seen before. With all those people in such a relatively small space, it's tempting to chat and get the scoop from the past weekend. Don't be surprised if you end up spending more time on study breaks than studying.

library research skills ~ assume you don't have any because the reality is you probably don't. The fancy microfiches and microfilm machines could be overwhelming and there will be lots of them. You will save tons of time and effort by asking the librarian for help.

lifetime learner ~ the adult in your class who will be the only student to show up for every single session. This grown up is usually the one to do all the reading and ready to answer any question the professor asks.

lil brother/lil sister ~ what your big brother or big sister calls you. Also, what you'll eventually have in a year or two when new members join. You'll be their big bro/big sis and your "family" will grow.

line dances ~ the challenge of dancing to the tune of *the Electric Slide* and actually staying in line formation.

loans ~ repeat after me: "Since I'll be in debt for a very long time and have to repay the loans plus interest, I will get my money's worth now and attempt to go to all my classes." Now that you're convinced to actually go to class, wouldn't it be a waste to go if you didn't do any work? Get into it. Who knows, you may really like it!

locker ~ no more lockers to shove all of your books, coat and stuff! Consider your dorm an expanded locker.

loft ~ a tall wooden bed frame, especially useful in a small room with a high ceiling, which allows for extra space underneath it. Rooms usually don't come with lofts so you'll have to buy wood and make one yourself or have other students or your parents build one for you.

lost and found ~ chances are your school has one and chances are, your keys are not there! Always check your room first. They may be stuck in the keyhole of your door.

lounges ~ your dorm will have at least one of these rooms for hanging out or studying, usually located in the basement. There's a TV, a few lamps without lightbulbs and a bunch of outdated couches.

M

magna cum laude ~ like graduating cum laude, only better! Although the requirement could be different at each school, it's usually a final cumulative GPA between 3.65 and 3.80.

mail ~ it doesn't matter how many friends you had in high school. The only real mail you get will be from your parents. A word or two about internet shopping: beware and be wired! As long as you can resist spending a lot of money with the click of your mouse, it is really fun ordering stuff. Consider it one way to guarantee you'll get a package in the mail!

mailbox ~ you'll check it everyday, sometimes more than once. Real mail is scarce but you can always count on getting fliers about campus events. See **wind tunnel**.

maintenance ~ these are the people in your neighborhood, the people that you meet walking down the street. They're the people who fix your radiator when it's blasting heat in September. Typically they'll knock at your door at the crack of dawn the one day you can actually sleep late.

major ~ the big kahuna, numero uno choice of your academic focus. You can go in to college with an undeclared major but you sure can't come out that way! You'll probably have to make this decision by sophomore year. Although everyone doesn't get a job in the Real World based on their major, most people start a career in an area that corresponded to their major. Here's a sample:

Psychology—social worker, teacher, PhD, human resources/personnel
English—teacher, social worker, writer, journalism, advertising
Bio—doctor, research analyst, nutritionist, nurse, dentist
Economics—accounting, financial analyst, investment banker, stock broker
Engineering—engineer, architect, surveyor
History—lawyer, politician, history teacher
Art—artist, art teacher, museum curator

"make grades" ~ expression used when referring to a certain GPA needed in order to be in good academic standing with the school. If you don't make grades (such as a minimum GPA of 2.0) then you may be placed on academic probation and not be able to participate in sports, Greek life, etc. The punishment all depends on your school's probation policy.

map ~ get one to avoid aimlessly walking around campus, looking like a clueless freshman.

march madness ~ the ultimate dream for any collegiate basketball player. The NCAA tourney (a.k.a. "the Big Dance") is the season's culmination of games when the nation's teams compete to be the very best in the country.

mardi gras ~ this may possibly be the grandest road trip of them all: Mardi Gras in New Orleans! Tons of people, jazz music and some good ol' fashion Creole cooking.

meal plan ~ concept of paying for meals you're not going to eat. Let's say it's mandatory to buy the plan with 20 meals each week. You'll end up missing meals here and there due to studying or social commitments. And when you do actually eat your meals on the plan, you'll wish you didn't. See **UFO.**

media ~ unlike your typical national tabloids, news or entertainment programs, colleges do their part with their school newspaper, literary magazines, radio and/or tv stations, humor magazines or underground papers.

memories ~ like the corners of my mind, scattered pictures...Many people say these are the best years of your life! Keep a journal, take pictures and do whatever you need to capture the moment in its full essence before it fades away.

message board ~ this wipe off board on your door is useful when your friends stop by and you're not around.

microfilm/fiche ~ if you didn't like these machines in the high school library, you surely won't like them now.

microphone ~ your professor uses this in a really, really big class so everyone can hear.

microwave ~ if you don't have one there's no need to worry 'cause someone on your floor will.

microwave popcorn ~ the ultimate study snack.

midterms ~ exams that occur halfway through the semester which are important but not a big deal in comparison to finals.

minor ~ a mini major. You'll get to focus on a subject but the courseload won't be as intense as your major.

mixers ~ parties between fraternities and sororities, usually held at the frat house. Yep, you've got your standard themes such as toga parties and

Halloween costume parties, but there are tons of other party ideas. Here's a sample:

Graffiti—the only prerequisite for this bash is wearing a clean, white t-shirt with the expectation that it will be written on during the party. You'll get a marker when the party starts so you can start writing on other people's t-shirts while they write on yours! The best part about this is reading your shirt the next day and having no idea who wrote what.

80s—there's nothing quite like reliving those 1980s fashion faux pas (like pinstripe jeans, legwarmers and sweater vests). The more dressed up people get, the better. Pop some early Madonna tunes in the stereo to really get into the groove.

My Tie—guys each put a tie in a huge box by the front door of their fraternity house. As girls arrive, they each take one tie out of the box and have to talk to different brothers throughout the night to determine who is the owner of the tie.

monday night football ~ yet another reason to party.

money ~ going out to dinner, movies, spending $300 on books for one semester. It's easy to spend and hard to save. This is where the part-time job comes in handy.

money back guarantee ~ there is none. Your money will not be refunded if you are not fully satisfied. Carpe diem! (Translation: seize the day!)

mononucleosis (mono) ~ illness that makes you feel completely exhausted. Since it's caused by being run down or by kissing someone who has it, it's no wonder why so many college students get mono.

moving in ~ act of making a ton of trips up and down the stairs, carrying your clothes and other stuff from your car into your new room. It's a grueling and sweaty event experienced by all of the family members you roped into this mess. (Believe me, you will need all of their help!)

moving out ~ the reverse of moving in, only now you have all this crap to bring home and nowhere to put it.

MTV ~ yet another fine way to procrastinate!

mudsliding ~ it's fun and crazy but it's definitely not clean! When it starts pouring rain, students run to the nearest hill and start sliding down it. Expect to get completely muddy and messy and be in need of a long shower. And the next stop after the shower stall? The laundry room, of course!

multiple guess ~ do this when you have no idea what the answer is to a multiple choice question. That is, take a wild guess!

munchies ~ late night craving for junk food like cheese fries. Usually occurs while studying or watching TV. See **freshman fifteen**.

N

names ~ you will know everyone on a first name basis. Last names will become obsolete. Instead, it'll be "Scott from English 101".

naps ~ are necessary. It's amazing what a little power nap can do for you, energizing you for the rest of the day. According to experts, the average college student requires 9 ¼ hours of sleep per night. Reality is you probably won't get a good night sleep every night so you'll do what every college student does for a quick fix: you'll nap! Keep your naps brief (less than one hour) in order to get refreshed. Keep in mind if you nap too late in the afternoon you'll have problems falling asleep at night.

national holidays ~ it's a major bummer when you check mail on days like President's Day and completely forget the post office is closed.

neat freak ~ person who maintains an incredibly clean and organized abode (in other words, the dorm room). This could be the cause of friction if you're a slob and your roomie is a neat freak or vice versa.

nerds ~ still exist. Even though you'll meet some really cool people who are also very smart, there will still be some guy in calc class wearing a pocket protector.

nicknames ~ you'll come to college without one, but you'll leave with one. Favorites include Buffy, Zeus and Thirsty.

the night before the first day of class ~ a big party night. It's one of the first times all the students will be on campus. Plus, there's no work to be done so it's prime time to socialize!

night classes ~ sound like a good thing at first until you realize it's usually once or twice a week for three hours a pop.

notebooks ~ a necessity for class. If you don't have time to get the notebooks at home before the semester starts, you can always buy notebooks in the bookstore with your school's name on it.

notes ~ take good ones. When you're studying, it's better to have too much info than not enough.

no worries ~ this is the only time in your life where your biggest troubles are studying for a chem exam and finding a decent formal date. Even though your hectic schedule will keep you on the go, in the big picture of life, this is the time to enjoy.

number ~ at a large university, your student ID number or social security number will be your identity on exams, papers and course registration.

O

office hours ~ times designated by your prof when he/she will be available in their office for consultation. Make an appointment to see your professor to review for an exam, discuss an upcoming paper topic or review an assignment you already submitted.

oktoberfest ~ theme party held in October that's a great excuse to wear silly hats and drink German beer.

on reserve ~ articles or assignments in the libes you can only borrow for a few hours at a time. Make copies of these articles so you have your own copy whenever you need it for reference.

"one-five" (as in, "I've got fives on this seat") ~ say this when you leave a room in order to save your seat for 15 minutes or until you return, whichever comes first. If you're not back in 15 minutes, the seat belongs to someone else.

one hundred nights ~ senior celebration that starts the countdown of 100 nights before the big G...Graduation!

open book exam ~ is just what it sounds like, but not as simple as you'd think. Bring all course material such as the textbook, notes and handouts and be prepared to take a few hours to complete it.

organic chemistry (a.k.a. "orgo") ~ this is what summer school is for. Some classes are too difficult to handle in addition to your regular courseload. This is one of them. Do the smart thing and take orgo in the summer.

orientation ~ the get-to-know-you week for freshmen before classes begin in the fall. Usually consists of corny ice breaker games, such as introducing yourself with an adjective that begins with the first letter of your first name, as in Darling Dave.

oversleep ~ yes, this can happen the day of a final. Set a back-up alarm.

P

packing ~ for freshman year, you'll spend weeks buying stuff, making lists of items and packing the car a week in advance. By senior year you'll bring only one-third of your belongings (if that!) and pack the day before you leave.

Here are some other things you'll bring but never use:

- Here are some other things AP Calc notebook from senior year—yeah, right. You know how hard it is to locate notes on exactly what you're looking for? It takes longer than reading your textbook!
- Thesaurus—why bother packing this book when Windows can look up a word for you!
- Cliffs Notes—they got you out of a jam in high school but that's where it ends.
- High school memorabilia—wake up. High school is over. Remember that thing called graduation? Time to move on and leave the hs yearbook at home with the 'rents.

Now that we got the don'ts out of the way, here are the do's. Here's a list of things to pack:

Academics
Computer, disks, desk lamp, lightbulbs, bulletin board, pens, highlighters, folders, notebooks, datebook/agenda, stapler, staples, scotch tape, scissors, dry erase marker, lap desk, backpack

Clothing

You're on your own with this one...

Eats

Mini-refrigerator, microwave, hot pot, snacks—microwave popcorn, soda, hard pretzels, etc.

Entertainment

TV, VCR, video tapes, stereo, CDs, cordless phone, answering machine, cell phone, walkman, batteries

Bed Stuff

Alarm clark, extra-long sheets, comforter, pillows,

Bathroom/Personal Products

Towels, robe, flip flops, bucket for the bathroom, toiletries—razor, soap, soap dish toothbrush and holder, toothpaste, shampoo, conditioner, deodorant, aspirin, tissues, cotton balls, Q-tips

Laundry Supplies

Laundry basket, detergent, fabric softener, measuring cup, quarters, drying rack

Decorative

Curtains, posters, fun tac, pictures

Comfort

Fan, backrest, fouton/Bean bag chair

Misc.

Clothes hangers, underbed storage, crates, carpet, garbage can, camera, batteries, film, extension cords, baseball hats

panhellenic council (a.k.a. PHC or panhel) ~ the governing body of sororities on campus. Panhel is made up of at least one member of each sisterhood on campus.

papers ~ get used to 'em and expect to do a whole lot of writing. Some homework assignments may be as little as three typed pages, whereas research papers may be 20 pages or more. If you're getting off to a slow start, talk to other students, a TA or your professor. It's better to get feedback to improve your paper before it's due than handing it in and getting it back with a comment like "needs work."

paper extensions ~ if you grovel enough, your professor may extend the due date of a paper. The downside is your grade may drop a level or two as a penalty for late submission.

parallel parking ~ get used to it. Even if you're not good at it, you'll become a pro. When the lots are full, parallel parking may become your only option.

parentals ~ mom and dad, the folks, the parents.

parents weekend/family day ~ campus event in the fall when the family visits you for the day or weekend, brings munchies for your room, goes to a football game and takes you to a restaurant for some real food.

parking permit ~ little sticker for your car window which means it's legit for your car to be on campus.

participation ~ raise that hand! Speak up in class! Be a total brain and get involved. If participating in class is factored into your final grade, open your mouth and talk. Who knows, you may actually enjoy it!

parties ~ whether it's a huge bash the last day of classes or a little get together with some people on your floor, it's time to socialize. Note: freshmen typically travel in packs of 20 to 30 people when walking to parties on campus. This happens in the beginning of the year when an entire hall will go out together. It's a lot of fun at first but a sure way for upperclassmen to spot the pack and know you're a frosh. As time goes on you'll go out with fewer people and closer friends, like a group of 8 to ten people.

the party dorm ~ fun place to visit but would you really want to live there? There are parties 24/7 with loud music, people lingering in the halls, not to mention the dirty bathrooms. Note: finding SpaghettiO's in the shower is not a good sign!

party mix ~ a tape of your favorite party tunes, especially useful when you throw a party.

pass/fail ~ earn credits for taking a class where the grade is not calculated into your GPA. Instead, you'll just get a P or an F. There are some restrictions such as not being able to take Pass/Fail for classes within your major or minor. Since you still have to study, it's a major bummer if you ace the class and it's not factored into your GPA.

pasta ~ a pretty safe meal to eat when other entrees make you queasy. Also, pasta is easy to make in your dorm with a hot pot.

peer counselors ~ just like the counseling center, peer counselors are fellow students who are there for you if you want to talk confidentially.

peer pressure ~ don't let it get the best (or worst!) of you.

performances ~ most colleges feature cheap entertainment that's really good. Use your student ID to see plays, musicians and comedians you'd otherwise pay big bucks for if you weren't a student.

petition ~ act of getting lots of signatures from your advisor, professors and a dean or two in order to get permission to double major, take a class at another school or study abroad, for instance.

pets ~ dogs, bunnies, ferrets, lizards, fish. You name it and chances are someone has this pet living in their little room. Most dorms prohibit animals but this doesn't always stop students from having them.

phi beta kappa ~ prestigious national honor society. Criteria is determined by the local chapter at each school, though you usually need really good grades and an invitation to join.

philanthropies ~ organizations raise money for important charities like the Juvenile Diabetes Foundation. Usually fraternities and sororities sponsor fundraising events for their charity such as a walk-a-thon.

phone calls ~ back home you might not call someone after 10 p.m., but calling someone on campus after midnight is not uncommon. Everyone's awake!

phone home ~ remember to call home every once in a while to say "hi" to the family.

phones ~ the public telephones on your floor are useful in the beginning of the school year before a phone line is installed in your room.

physical education (phys ed) ~ this is less grueling than your high school gym class. Typical classes are tennis or golf.

pictures ~ to some they are memories, to others they're evidence.

piercing ~ you may get the sudden urge to get an ear or body part pierced. Make sure the needle is clean, you sit very still and that you won't regret waking up with this random piece of jewelry on your body the next morning.

pigsty ~ the gigantic heap of sloppiness better known as your dorm room. This may cause tension if your roommate is a neat freak and you're a total slob or vice versa.

pinning ~ a pre-engagement event that creates another great reason for a party. A guy gives his fraternity pin to his girlfriend for her to wear on a necklace, symbolizing their serious relationship. Used in a sentence like this: "Jen and Chris got pinned this past weekend. I'm so happy for them!"

pizza ~ snack eaten at 2 a.m.

plaid couches ~ your parents old furniture actually serves a purpose and will be put to good use in your dorm.

play ~ time to have fun!

play hooky (that is, if you cut class) ~ ah, the beauty of college. If you skip class one day you don't necessarily need to skip all of your classes. Unlike high school where you'd be out one day and miss every single class, here you can skip your 8 or 9 a.m. but still make it to your 2 and 3 p.m.

pledge ~ person who accepts a bid from a fraternity or sorority but is not an official member yet. Pledging usually lasts six to eight weeks. During this time you'll learn the history of the organization, meet all the members and have tons of fun or otherwise grueling tasks, like cleaning the bathroom floor with your toothbrush.

pledge class ~ group of people who get their bids at the same time, spend a lot of time together and do some major bonding.

pledge pack ~ the "goody bag" pledges carry with them at all times. Some fraternities or sororities give pledges a list of things they have to carry with them at all times like a pack of gum, postage stamps or quarters for laundry.

pocketbook/purse ~ one sure way to spot freshwomen. Look like an upperclassman and ditch that purse! (Simply shove everything into your backpack.)

pong ~ short for ping pong, this old-fashioned table tennis game is cool again. For the 21 year-old crowd, the game is actually called "beer pong". Strategically place cups of beer on the pong table and let the games begin! If you hit the ball off of your opponent's cup, they have to take a sip but if you hit it into your opponent's cup, they have to chug!

poor ~ as in, you will be. By paying for your books, eating dinners out and munching on late night eats, it's easy to go through money really, really fast. Make sure to work hard in the summer and save up.

pop quizzes ~ happen. But are they really necessary? If professors tell you on the first day of class to expect them, take the hint and do all of the reading assignments.

popularity ~ no longer exists. Hallelujah! In high school you had your typical cliques, including the popular kids. Welcome to college, where there is no concept of popularity. If there is the slightest sense of an "in" crowd it doesn't really matter if you don't hang with them.

porcelain god ~ used in a sentence like this: "I got so wasted on my twenty-first birthday I ended up hugging the porcelain god."

posters ~ there's no need to buy any. The most popular and cheapest wall decor is tearing out Absolut ads from magazines.

potential formal date (otherwise known as "PFD") ~ people you would consider asking to be your formal date. College etiquette dictates that you give your date no more than two weeks notice. Asking any sooner would be a major faux pas (too over anxious). Asking a few days before the big night is plenty of time.

power nap ~ a nap taken for a very brief amount of time such as fifteen minutes. You'd be amazed at how refreshed you can feel after one of these.

pranks ~ are you really surprised that 350 portions of chicken chimichangas are missing from the caf?

pre-parties ~ talking, drinking, dancing and singing; basically hanging out with your friends before going to a party.

prerequisite ~ course you must take in order to take a higher level class. For example, the prereq for Social Psychology is Psychology 101. Most of your freshman year will be made of 101 classes.

presentations ~ usually occur at the very end of the semester when you have a bizillion assignments due for every class. These require a lot of research and those public speaking abilities you wish you had.

privacy ~ yeah, right. The walls are thin and rumors fly. See **gossip**.

probation ~ also known as "pro." Academic pro, warning pro, social pro, you name it and they've got it. Try to be good because you won't want to be underage at a party with a beer in your hand when security comes.

procrastination ~ you will do too much of this. Which would you rather do: check e-mail or read 200 pages of British Lit?

Here's a little list of pointers to avoid the procrastination bug.

- Get out of your dorm. It's way too tempting to sit in your room, staring at the tv, your cd collection and the phone. Go to the library. Study in the lounge or find an empty classroom in an academic building to get away from those dorm room distractions.
- So you've found a place to study, just make sure it's not too comfy. This is not the time for a power nap!
- The more you do now the less you have to do later. It seems so easy to blow things off now, but it's not until you've pulled your first all-nighter, cursing at yourself to the point where you can't concentrate any more, that you'll learn the true price of procrastination.

proctor ~ faculty member or grad student who supervises an exam. Also, this is a person at the computer lab who can assist you if you need help.

productive procrastination ~ instead of procrastinating by watching TV or playing computer games, you procrastinate by actually accomplishing something else, such as cleaning your room.

professors ~ these intellects split their time between teaching and doing research. Note: never call them Mr. or Ms.; instead, put professor in front of their name such as Professor Taylor. If they have a PhD, it's a whole new ballgame. See **doctor**.

programs ~ depending on your school, there will probably be speakers lecturing on campus each week. Whether it's foreign policy or cultural

implications of *the Brady Bunch*, find out who's coming to campus. It will be well worth your time.
provost ~ after four years of college you will still have no idea what this person in administration does.

psychology experiments ~ volunteer, be a subject and you can say you contributed to the advancement of science.

Q

the quad ~ a square field in the center of campus which is absolutely the best place to toss a frisbee or sit under a tree on a sunny spring day. But wait, that's not all! As opposed to "the quad", "a quad" is a living arrangement with two double rooms joined by a bathroom.

quarters ~ you'll need these to do your laundry. Plus, at the beginning of the school year before your phone is installed you'll need spare change to make calls from the pay phone on your floor.

quiet hours ~ dorm rules upheld during finals limiting you and your neighbors from blasting music and making lots of noise. If quiet hours begin at midnight, students are supposed to keep noise to a minimum from midnight until the morning.

quote boards ~ a posterboard you and your roomie write on to record your inside jokes and remember those outrageous times from the entire year.

R

raffles ~ you'll spend money like water and it will go towards things like this. They're usually for charity and hey, you may even win a prize!

the rain ~ sucks. Don't bother doing your hair.

random ~ include this word in your college vocabulary 'cause you'll use it all the time: "For lunch they served hotdogs and omelets. That's so random."

ratio ~ male/female student ratio. While parents are interested in the student/faculty ratio at your school, you'll be more interested in this one.

reading ~ you will never *ever* do so much of this. For each class you may expect to read a few hundred pages each week. Keep up with your reading because falling behind is a fate worse than death! It's next to impossible to catch up because you'll have new reading assignments in addition to the ones you blew off.

reading day ~ the day after classes end, but before finals begin. Most students spend the day reviewing their notes and forming study groups to prepare for exams.

the real world ~ don't even think about it. You don't have a curfew, all your friends are within walking distance and you can take naps in the middle of the day.

recycling bins ~ never before have colleges been so environmentally correct.

red tape ~ obstacles that make life difficult, better known as the administration.

refrigerator ~ this mini frig is 1/3 the size of a real one, yet big enough for all your needs (random stuff like orange juice, leftover Chinese food and mustard). This bulky item makes life difficult when moving into/out of your dorm.

registrar's office ~ the office in charge of keeping track of your major, courses, credits, grades and graduation requirements.

registration ~ how you sign up for classes is different at each school. Yours might be via the telephone, on the web or by completing paperwork and standing on line at the Registrar's office. No matter how your school does it, take it seriously, do it early, allow plenty of time and select alternate courses in case the ones you want are full.

rentals ~ instead of buying big ticket items you can rent things like a computer or refrigerator.

the 'rents ~ your parents.

requirements ~ courses in your major you must take. Make sure you're on the right track before junior year or else you'll be on the five year plan.

research ~ you may want to do this for a professor during your junior or senior year. Whether it's paid work or not, it always looks good on a resume.

resident advisor (RA) ~ your pseudo parent/friend/big bro/big sis who is a little bit older and a little bit wiser. They live in each dorm and there's usually one or two on each floor. Talk to them if you're homesick, have roomie troubles or simply just to chat.

residence hall ~ nice way of saying a dorm.

resume ~ a single sheet of paper that documents your work experience, education and skills.

rho chi ~ a rush counselor. This person is assigned to groups for sorority rushing and helps rushees make decisions about which house to join.

rhodes scholarship ~ prestigious study abroad in which only 32 students from the US are selected to study at Oxford University in England.

ride board ~ post your name on a bulletin board, usually online or in the student center and hopefully you'll connect with someone going your way.

road trip ~ because every once in a while we all need to get away. Even if it's visiting a friend at another school or going to your roommate's home for the weekend, sometimes a little break is all you need.

robe ~ when you live on a co-ed floor, sometimes you won't want to be seen wearing just a towel.

"rocks for jocks" ~ even classes have nicknames! This one is known as Geology 101 in the course catalog.

rollerblading ~ who says you have to walk to class?

room ~ your on-campus digs will be equipped with a desk, dresser and bed. You'll decorate it, make it cozy, build a loft and call it home.

room and board ~ fee to live in your dorm and pay for the meal plan.

roommate ~ The one, the only: the roommate. When you find out your freshman dorm assignment, you should contact your new roomie to introduce yourself and get all the important matters out of the way, like who is bringing what. The major things should be discussed so you don't both end up bringing your monster stereo. Here's a little list of items to talk about: carpet, refrigerator, microwave, curtains, phone, answering machine, TV and VCR. Just remember you don't have to be best buds with your roomie; all you have to do is live with this person. Be courteous, take phone messages when they're not around and don't play music when they're studying. It's as simple as that.

room picks ~ process of selecting a room for next year which is different at each school. See **housing lottery**.

ROTC ~ acronym for Reserve Officer Training Corps, in which students receive military training and experience as undergrads.

rush ~ the process of Greek membership selection. The goal is to meet lots of brothers or sisters, get to know several houses and eventually find a house with really cool people. Girls usually attend rounds of parties at the sorority houses and watch slide shows while guys hang out at several houses for events like Monday Night Football. Meanwhile, the goal for the house is to get to know all the rushees and eventually get the really cool people to join. Basically if everyone meets awesome people (the rushee meets a great house and the house meets a fantastic potential member), then everyone's happy!

S

SATs ~ seem pretty senseless now, huh?

saturday finals ~ can happen to you. It really stinks, mainly because who wants to wake up on a Saturday to take an exam? More importantly, who wants to study on a Friday night?

scammer ~ total slimeball. This person is likely to cheat on his hometown.

scavenger hunt ~ a game where you search for various items based on a series of clues. For example, two orientation groups may have to do a series of things, such as taking a picture with the school mascot. The group that finishes first with the most items wins.

schedules ~ classes shouldn't interfere with your sleep. Schedule your classes wisely and you, too, can sleep in on weekdays! In other words, if a class is given at 2 p.m. and at 8 a.m., do the right thing. Sign up for that 2 o'clock class! You may not always get your first choice, but at least you'll know you didn't get that 8 a.m. class as a result of your own self-inflicted torture.

scholarships ~ discounts on high tuition costs in the forms of grants, financial aid, etc.

school ~ unlike any other school you've attended, this time in August you'll actually be excited to go back!

school bus ~ not just for elementary school anymore. Now it's a mode of transportation to the formal (usually held off-campus at a hotel or bar/restaurant) and other off-campus events such as away football games.

school decal ~ nifty decal or sticker of your school's name in big letters. Must be fastened to your car's rear window for all to see!

school spirit ~ go team, go! Yep, you had your pep rallies in high school, big football games and homecoming, your college will have all these and more!

scope ~ to check someone out, especially useful when searching for a PFD. Creative scoping methods include going to the gym, hanging out in the student center or going to the libes on a Sunday night.

scrapbook ~ make one and capture all those special moments using pictures and quotes. You'll regret it if your only memories consist of sleep deprivation from all-nighters and cramming sessions that put you out of commission for days.

screw your roommate ~ party in which roommates set each other up on blind dates.

sections or sessions ~ a multiple offering of classes. Instead of having one gigantic class, the class is broken into sections and is given several times a week. For instance, Biology 101 might be given on M, W, F at 8 a.m., 10 a.m. and 2 p.m.

security ~ people employed at your school for security reasons. Consider them an on-campus police squad.

self-portraits ~ are great fun. They're crazy, they're close up and if you're lucky, they may even be centered.

selling your books ~ end of semester ritual of selling the $75 textbook you bought just a few months ago back to the bookstore for $10. It's an easy way to earn cash, but not a whole lot of it. If a new edition is released and updates were made to your textbook, your book will be worth even less. In this case you should consider keeping some books for future reference.

semesters (fall and spring) ~ what you used to call "marking periods".

senior week ~ the final hoorah and week long celebration before hard-earned diplomas are granted.

senior year ~ ask any senior and they'll either tell you that senior year is a blast and you party every night or you completely stress about the future. Note: never ask a senior what their plans are for after graduation. If he/she knows what they're doing, they will tell you voluntarily.

senioritis ~ itchiness to graduate when you've had enough of the exams, all-nighters, cafeteria food and parties (yes, even the parties get old after four years).

shopping for class ~ sitting in classes, getting the syllabus and checking out the professors in the beginning of the semester when you're not sure what classes to take. Oh yeah—shopping is over when the Registrar's office says it's over. See **drop/add.**

shopping days ~ the countdown of remaining days until the formal. It's the number of days left to shop for a formal date and ask him/her to go with you.

shorts ~ it may be August, it may be mid-February but it doesn't really matter. Your dorm will blast heat all year so you'll end up wearing shorts no matter what the weather is outside.

shuttle ~ transportation used at some big universities to drive you across campus very quickly.

silverware ~ there's no need to buy utensils. And guess what? There's no need to wash them either. Take clean silverware from the caf and use it. When you're done, return it to the caf in the dirty silverware bin and someone else will clean it for you. It's a pretty creative concept to recycle silverware and never have to wash it.

single ~ if you don't have a roomie, you live in a single.

sisters ~ members of a sorority.

sleep ~ you can never get enough.

snooze button ~ you loved it in high school, you'll love it now.

snowball fights ~ because you're never too old to play in the snow.

snowstorms ~ there are two very important points to remember: classes won't be canceled if your profs live near school and cafeteria trays make awesome sleds!

social life ~ it will be never so easy to have one again. All your friends are within walking distance and there's always something happening on campus or off.

social living group ~ a bunch of people who live together or in the same building, floor or dorm who also share a common interest.

social studies ~ has grown up and now it's called "history". Also, "social studies" occurs when you're in the libes totally procrastinating by talking to your friends when you should be studying.

songs ~ sooner or later someone will teach you a crazy chant or two or ten. Don't ask who makes up these silly songs about your school, just be sure to belt them out as loud as you can!

sophomore blues ~ you may hit this little slump during sophomore year. Freshman year is new and exciting so it's inevitable that your second year may be a bit of a let-down. Since college goes by way too fast to be depressed, just acknowledge it and move on.

sophomore year ~ you'll know your campus pretty well by now, who your friends are, where to hang out and how to get the most out of college by balancing the fine art of studying and having an active social life.

sorority ~ group of girls in a Greek organization with secret rituals, officers and meetings. Sororities also sponsor fundraisers and go to mixers. Typically members form strong friendships and become close like sisters.

spell check ~ because professors don't like typos.

spring break ~ oh yeah! Party by night and recover on the beach by day. Favorites include Daytona Beach, Cancun or Jamaica. Mon.

spring fever ~ triggered by the first warm day in the spring, pong tables and plaid couches get moved to the quad and everyone is outside hanging out. No matter how hard you try, it's impossible to study.

statues ~ big replicas of people who founded your school, as well as the mascot. These statues are placed throughout campus and are likely to be pelted with eggs or spray paint when the rival team comes to town for the big game.

stereo ~ there's always one person who has the loudest stereo on campus and blasts the tunes from their room. If you live down the hall from this person, let's hope you like their taste in music!

"the stride of pride" ~ for anyone who hooked up in someone else's room, you gotta get back to your room somehow! Briskly walk home at the crack of dawn to avoid seeing anyone you know. This hike across campus is either called "the stride of pride" or "the walk of shame" depending on how your night went.

student center/student union ~ the place to be. Usually the cafeteria, mailroom, bookstore and activity offices are here but the main purpose is to put in face time. It ultimately serves as a social place to hang out with friends and scope for that PFD.

study ~ act of reading and immersing yourself in books, lectures, labs and learning.

study abroad ~ let the world be your classroom! Study at another school, travel, experience another culture, learn another language and make new friends. For the most comprehensive programs available, read *Peterson's Study Abroad* which is updated every year. This book addresses everything on your mind like class credit, destinations, international internships, volunteer opportunities as well as financial considerations and living on a budget.

study break ~ the break you take from studying. Eating and walking around the libes are some examples. Just be sure your breaks don't last longer than your studying!

study buddy ~ someone you study with from your class.

study hours ~ like the study halls you had in high school but this time you will actually get work done. Some clubs have mandatory hours to encourage students to study for a specific amount of time like 7-9 p.m. Mondays in the **libes.**

study rooms ~ soundproof rooms in libraries provide a secluded place for your study group to meet. You'll probably have to reserve this room ahead of time with the library.

student discounts ~ save moolah on haircuts, movies, museums and other good stuff just by showing your school ID.

substitute teachers ~ no more subs! Unlike high school, you'll rarely have a sub if your professor can't make it to class.

suitcase school ~ school with a non-existent social scene. On Friday afternoons, all the students bolt outta there and the campus is quiet and empty for the entire weekend.

summa cum laude ~ your grades should only be this awesome. At most schools if you graduate with a GPA that's higher than 3.80, you can forever say that you graduated with this distinction.

summers ~ long break useful for job internships, visiting friends,traveling and most of all, relaxing!

sundays ~ the day to buckle down considering you haven't opened a book since Friday.

supersoaker (mega water gun) ~ because college kids like water sports.

syllabus ~ the schedule of reading assignments, projects and exams for the entire semester.

syllabus day ~ supposedly on the first day of classes all you do is show up at class to get the syllabus and leave. Do not be fooled, my friend. This doesn't happen anymore because the first day of class is serious stuff. Plan to sit through a lecture and take notes.

T

t-shirts ~ at $10 each, you'll buy at least one during your first semester. It's hard to resist buying from people who go door-to-door selling shirts with your school's name on it and sayings like "Co-ed Naked Lacrosse: rough, tough and in the buff".

tailgate ~ hanging out and roasting some hot dogs in the parking lot before the big game.

take home exam ~ sure, it sounds easy. But if it were, do you really think the professor would let you take it home?

tardy slips ~ there's no need for late slips or parents excuses in college. If you're late to class you should quietly enter the classroom and make as little commotion as possible. Depending on how late you oversleep, you might consider not even going at all. See **play hooky**.

tar beach ~ porch roofs of fraternity or sorority houses used for basking in the sun.

tattoos ~ same concept as piercing in which you need to make a serious decision to ensure you won't regret waking up with the Tasmanian Devil on your arm the next morning.

teaching assistant (TA) ~ upperclass or graduate students who teach a lab or grade papers.

ten minute rule ~ this unofficial rule is not stated specifically in any course materials or college handbook, but if you ask students they know the drill. If the professor doesn't show up within the first ten minutes of class, it is OK for the students to leave.

Thanksgiving ~ four day weekend that provides the nice little break before the semester kicks into high gear and you have tons of assignments, papers, presentations and exams for all your classes.

thesis ~ huge research paper done by a junior or senior in order to graduate with honors or simply to graduate! Some schools make writing a thesis optional while others make it a graduation requirement.

Thursday ~ the official start of the weekend. Friday classes are merely a technicality.

time ~ really does fly. Start that lab report now!

time management ~ the key to success. Prioritize your schedule and make sure you can do it all without getting stressed out.

toga ~ brings new meaning to the word "party". Just wrap a sheet around yourself and you're good to go.

topographical map room ~ room that exists in almost every library even though you'll have no idea where it is or what it's for.

toss the cookies ~ to yak, hurl, or in simple terms, to puke.

tour guide ~ student who knows the ins and outs of your campus and gives tours to perspective students and their parents. This person walks backwards showing off the school's major attractions, like the academic buildings, the dorms and of course, the campus bookstore.

tours ~ seem so weird! Just the other day you were observing college life and suddenly you're immersed in it. And remember, as long as there are windows on classroom doors, there will be parents poking their heads in.

townies ~ the locals of any college town. You can spot a townie a mile away if they're on campus. Not to stereotype or anything, but they're typically older than a college student. Some are grizzly looking—picture a man with a thick long beard, five tattoos and four teeth.

transfers ~ typically they're sophomores or juniors who transfer from another school, but getting used to your campus makes them born again freshmen.

triple ~ having a triple room means you'll have not one but two roommates.

Tuesday ~ the day you should do your laundry. Or Mondays or Wednesdays or any time during the week when people are in class and the dorms are empty. Sundays are typically the most crowded because the weekend activities are over and no one has any clean clothes for the upcoming week.

tuition ~ fee to attend school, usually a hefty one. See **loans**.

tupperware ~ a creative way to hoard food from the cafeteria and prevent it from going stale.

tutors ~ your new found friends. Anyone who's willing to help you understand Regression Analysis and prevent you from failing is a friend indeed!

TV ~ almost everyone has one and a VCR plus a collection of videos to watch on a rainy Sunday afternoon.

twenty-four/seven (24/7) ~ anything done all day, every day. "You can tell it's finals because I'm studying 24/7."

U

UFO ~ unidentifiable food object. It's always best to make sure you can see what you're eating. Ordering an egg roll, stromboli or anything that's hidden inside a shell is not wise.

umbrella ~ the ultimate faux pas. It's much better to run across the quad and get a little wet than be seen carrying an umbrella.

underbed storage ~ these boxes add a new dimension to your limited closet space.

undergraduate ~ anyone enrolled in a college or university to earn their bachelor's degree. In other words, yourself!

underground ~ name given to a Greek organization or club such as a school newspaper that exists but doesn't receive funding or acknowledgment from the school.

unlimited local calls ~ all those campus calls can get expensive if you pay for each one individually. When you sign up for phone service, request to have one monthly payment that will cover the local calls regardless of how many you make.

V

vegetables ~ now that you're away from home do you think you're really going to eat broccoli? Ha! Seriously though, if you think you can survive on burgers and cheese fries, think again. Without sounding preachy you'll need some serious fruit and veggies to give you energy and important nutrients your body craves.

visiting hours ~ time designated in some dorms when members of the opposite sex are not allowed to visit, basically meaning they can't stop by whenever they want.

visits home ~ convenient way to do your laundry for free and stock up on snacks like pretzels. See the 'rents and siblings and escape from your hectic world, even if it is only for one weekend.

vitamins ~ little pills your mom bought for you because she knows you won't eat all your veggies. Though you probably won't take these little poppers, you'll inevitably get run down and need to visit the health center.

vocabulary ~ words you used in high school are now considered passé. Take a peek at the words you used to use on a daily basis and your new and improved vocab:

Then	*Now*
marking period	semester
teacher	professor
test	exam

report card	grades
vacation	break
homeroom	there is no homeroom, silly!

voicemail/answering machine ~ because you'll be in class, the libes, the student center, the gym, down the hall hanging with friends and you won't want to miss those important calls.

W

waitlist ~ your name is put on this list when you sign up for a class that already has the maximum number of students enrolled in it. If your name is high on the waitlist, you might get in. But chances are, if the class if full it's a popular class everyone wants to take so few people will drop it.

"the walk of shame" ~ for anyone who hooked up in someone else's room, you gotta get back to your room somehow! Briskly walk home at the crack of dawn to avoid seeing anyone you know. This hike across campus is either called "the walk of shame" or "the stride of pride" depending on how your night went.

walking ~ plan to do a lot of it. You'll be all over the place in the course of one day so you should get comfy sneakers.

watch ~ wear one *tous les temps* (that's French for "all the time"). Time flies fast enough so you might as well be aware of it.

water ~ water fountains in your hall may not be bad for a little sip, but if you're really thirsty you should buy the bottled stuff instead. Some H_20 fountains are old and have crusty pipes and not-so-fresh water. Ewwww.

weekends ~ are one big blur. You party, you sleep. You party, you sleep. Next thing you know it's Monday morning.

well lit ~ don't expect the campus to be. Walk with friends or call security to escort you home.

"what's up with that?" Generic saying you can use in any situation at any time. "We took the midterm three weeks ago and we still haven't gotten our grades. What's up with that?"

the wind ~ sucks. Don't bother styling your hair.

wind tunnel ~ an empty mailbox. After experiencing the wind tunnel day after day, you'll stop checking mail daily and only do it a few times a week.

wired ~ you're hyper, you're giddy, you're bouncing off the walls. After all, it's 4 a.m., you've had three cups of coffee and you're cruising through your notes on Macroeconomics. Be careful; it's only a matter of time before you **crash**.

work, work, work ~ college is not all fun and games.

work/study ~ if you're on financial aid, you will probably have a campus job like working in the libes. Your paycheck can go towards paying tuition or expenses.

X

xerox ~ machine used to make copies when you miss class and have to borrow someone's notes.

Y

year ~ you will have friends who are older and younger than you so it doesn't matter what grade you are in, however one of the first questions asked when you meet someone is, "What year are you?"

yearbook ~ you had one in high school and guess what? You'll get one now too. The only difference is, people won't sign it and you'll only buy it senior year.

yesterday ~ you'll do so many things in one day that everything you did yesterday will seem like such a long time ago!

yoga ~ yes, you can sign up for a class like this. It may be a gym class or simply an activity held at night or early morning. Others are scuba diving, tennis and golf.

Z

zany ~ you're only young once so be silly if you feel like it and skip across campus if the mood strikes!

Juicy Stuff

But wait, there's more! Now that you've got the lingo down to a science we can't forget the school-specific take on **the ABC's**: the traditions, tales, and pranks that make campus life come alive.

Activities

A cappella Appeal

Sure there are typical clubs like student government and the newspaper on every campus but a wave of cool a cappella groups are taking the nation's campuses by storm. With fun names like the Cords, Chaos and the Jabberwocks, these singing groups (sans instruments) are belting out classics from the 1950's Earth Angel to current hits on the pop charts.

The oldest female collegiate a cappella group in the nation, Smith College's very own Smiffenpoofs, was originated in 1936 after Smith College women attended a Smith-Yale picnic in which Yale's a cappella group, the Whiffenpoofs performed.

Hoyas Dance Sport

If you think ballroom dancing is just for older adults wearing swanky costumes, think again. At Georgetown University, home of the Hoyas, the hot campus activity is the Georgetown Ballroom Dance Club. Moving to the beat, they get down with swing dancing, latin dancing like the mambo and the cha-cha, and ballroom dancing such as the tango waltz and the foxtrot. The competitive team, Hoyas Dance Sport, practices two hours each week in order to train for competitions on the local, national and international level.

Activities Fair

Roo Fair

At the University of Missouri at Kansas City, the annual activities fair is so huge it's called the Roo Fair, named after their mascot Kasey the Kangaroo! Over 200 organizations are represented at the Roo Fair, in which students can sign up for different activities.

After Hours

Late Night Beans

Some students burning the midnight oil run to get coffee while others fuel up on snacks. It's a completely different picture for students at Bowdoin because they run out to go shopping! It's not uncommon for students at Bowdoin College in Brunswick, Maine to go on Late Night Bean Runs (that is, they go shopping at L.L. Bean which is open 24 hours a day, 365 days a year!)

Animal House

Did somebody say TOGA?

Get this. National Lampoon's *Animal House* was filmed in 1978 and depicted college as one huge toga party at Faber College. Although Faber is a fictitious institution, rumor has it that it was based on life at Dartmouth College.

Athletics

"Rolling the Quad"

At Wake Forest University, after the sports team has a victorious game, students race back to campus and throw toilet paper all over trees on the quad.

"Tenting"

Students at Duke University have a unique way of camping out prior to a big basketball game. Rather than waiting in line the old fashioned way for tickets, they actually assemble tents weeks so people can hang out and party as they wait for their turn to get tickets.

Bands

Notre Dame Victory March

The Band of the Fighting Irish, the official marching band of the University of Notre Dame, is the oldest university band in existence. Founded in the 1840s, this band is known for having performed at every home football game at Notre Dame since 1887! The kick off of a football weekend begins with a traditional pep rally on Friday night. The band musters students with a march throughout campus and arrives as the head of parade of the Irish faithful at the campus' Joyce Center. The band is known for belting out the Alma Mater ("Notre Dame, Our Mother") and the Notre Dame Victory March ("Cheer, cheer for old Notre Dame").

Bid Day

Bridge of the Bids

At the College of William and Mary in Virginia, the country's oldest institution, on sorority acceptance day all the pledges must cross a bridge barricaded by fraternity men.

Big Sis/Lil Sis

Dink Donut Night

Not only do sororities have big sisters and lil sisters, but women's colleges typically have a Big Sis program so freshwomen get to meet upperclasswomen. Every fall Cedar Crest College in Pennsylvania, junior and sophomore big sisters create dinks, old-time college beanies for their little sisters. The night is filled with donut eating contests, dink decorating contests and dancing.

Birthdays

It's so much friendlier with two!

At the University of Texas at Austin, an annual event is held each year in a park to celebrate a gloomy donkey's birthday. Eeyore's birthday is celebrated every year by thousands of revelers who dress up for costume contests and listen to live bands in honor of Winnie-the-Pooh's one and only dreary donkey.

Bizarre buildings

"I'm going to study in the John"

Students at Brown University nicknamed The Rockefeller Library "The Rock". It was named in honor of John D. Rockefeller, a benefactor of Brown. At first campus administrators weren't too pleased with the unrespectful shortening of his name. They got over it pretty fast because it was much better than what some students began calling the library: "the John".

Blow off class

Unofficial (and uncensored!) Guides to College

Wanna know the easiest class to take at Rutgers? Or how about the best dorm to live in at Penn State? And what about the Huskies favorite place to get a bite to eat at UConn? Introducing *The Students' Unofficial Guide to College*, several books of best and worsts for students at universities like Rutgers, Penn State, UConn and UMass. Never before has stuff been revealed like the biggest blow off class, the best club to join, biggest party mishap and favorite sport to watch at a particular school. Each book is based on write-in surveys from thousands of students. In fact, the Rutgers book became the fastest selling trade book in the history of Rutgers University!

Cafeteria

The Cool Rat

Although a rathskellar is the old-time college word for a small college cafeteria, to students at the Florida Institute of Technology, the Rat is actually a cool hangout. Students go there to play pool, watch the big screen TV and munch on burgers and fries.

Campus

Origin of the word

Way back in the olden days of the 1700s, American universities called the grounds around their buildings a yard or a green. It wasn't until the late 1700s that Jonathan Witherspoon, the president of Princeton University, coined the term "campus" to describe the large fields around Nassau Hall, a prominent building at Princeton.

Campus events

Annual Art Attack

At the University of Maryland, students know the drill. Work hard, play hard and at the end of the spring semester, dance and frolic at the Art Attack. This annual campus-wide music festival has been frequented by the *MTV "Campus Invasion Tour"* in the past. In addition to famous performers, there's a stage for dancing and singing, carnival rides and activities like a giant slide, a velcro wall and human foosball.

Canceled class

Cold cancellation

Forget about snowstorms, hurricanes or tornadoes being powerful enough to cancel class. At Colby College in Maine, classes have been known to be canceled due to the freezing boilers. Much to the administration's chagrin, students think it's pretty *cool.*

Careers

Gateway to the Future

At Lafayette College in Pennsylvania, students begin to plan for their future as early as freshman year as part of the Gateway Program. This four-year career development plan consists of providing a wide range of informational and counseling services to students. Each student is paired up with a professional career advisor who will work out an action plan based on the student's interests and goals. Available resources include an extensive network of alumni who provide internships, a comprehensive library, job search methods, mock interviews, resume critiques, on-campus interviews and video conferencing interviews with potential employers. In addition, students are linked to a computerized job database, which will send them a notification when the career office receives information about a job vacancy that matches their skills.

Class Rings

Class Ceremonies

So we already established the fact that you're not going to wear your high school ring, but how about a collegiate piece of jewelry? At some schools, you simply buy the ring through the bookstore and get it in the mail; at other schools formal ring ceremonies are held. For instance, at the College of Charleston, the ring has a copyrighted official design which features the college seal in a round signet. The ring is available to degree holders and to students who have completed at least sixty credit hours. Ring receptions are held twice each year, once in the fall semester and once in the spring and get this, rings are presented to each student by the college president!

Commencement Bingo

Bingo was his Name-O

At Stephens College, seniors have been known to have a mock commencement in which students play bingo by marking off their bingo cards after hearing keywords like "future" and "opportunity".

Dance Marathon

Rock til ya Drop

Students at Penn State University bring this to a new level with THON, an annual 48-hour dance marathon, the largest student fundraiser in the world! This IFC/Panhellenic dance marathon is so well organized it actually has an Overall Morale Committee to get the dancers prepared emotionally, mentally and physically to become a 48-hour dancing machine. Members of campus organizations get involved and alumni come back to participate to raise money for The Four Diamonds Fund, Conquering Childhood Cancer. Over a span of thirty years, this fundraiser has raised $16 million!

Elections

Rock the vote

Here's the deal. People fought really hard to make this country a free place where our voices can be heard. In order to help young people utilize their power to affect change, Rock the Vote was developed to protect freedom of expression. Originally founded by members of the recording industry, it's website www.rockthevote.org has important info like what's going on in the economy, crime & violence, censorship, civil rights, education, political reform and the environment. And for those of you who missed the last election, you have no excuse. You can register to vote on-line!

Politics as usual

Many schools, such as Vanderbilt University in Tennessee, have several campus organizations relating to politics and promote voting such as the College Democrats, College Republicans, Vanderbilt Green Party, Vanderbilt Civil Liberties Union, and the Vanderbilt International Politics Club.

Electives

Just Clowning Around

In the theater department at the University of Virginia, students get serious when it comes to clowning around especially when they take a course taught by Professor LaVohn Hoh. Hoh, a nationally known circus historian, teaches the only accredited course in the nation on the history of the

American circus. He's also an archivist for Ringling Bros. and Barnum & Bailey Clown College.

E-mail

You've got mail

Dartmouth's e-mail on campus is known as blitz mail. Before and after class students sit in front of their computer and check their "blitzes". It's not uncommon for students to "blitz" each other with the latest weekend plans.

Finals

AAAAAAAAAAhhhhhhhhhhhhhhhhhh

At Boston College in Massachusetts, every night during finals, students can be found studying, stressing, and um...screaming. At 11 p.m., students follow the BC tradition of leaning out of their dorm windows and collectively screaming for about twenty minutes.

Talk about superstitions!

At Miami University in Oxford, Ohio students carefully walk on the slant walk, a sidewalk with the school's emblem engraved on it. As they walk they avoid stepping on the seal. Legend has it if you step on the seal you will fail your final exams!

Good Luck Ritual

On a lighter note, women at Bryn Mawr leave votives around the base of the statue Athena Lemnia as a sign for good luck on exams.

Streaking Tradition

On the last day of classes in spring but before finals begin, students at University of Michigan take it off. Check that, they take it all off. In an attempt to perpetuate the tradition, students run naked through Ann Arbor Michigan as part of the annual Naked Mile.

Founders Day

Lucky Number Thirteen

Colgate University in New York has a rather unique relationship with the number 13. Apparently thirteen baptist men with thirteen prayers and thirteen dollars founded the university in 1819. In fact, Colgate observes thirteen traditions today, one of which is placing thirteen chairs on the platform for major convocations.

Freshmen

Old-time Hazefest

First-year students used to be called greenies, plebes or scrubs by upperclassmen in the 1900s. Though it would be called hazing now, the upperclassmen used to make the freshman class wear beanies on their head or a green ribbon to signify they were freshmen. They often ran errands for upperclassmen just because they were frosh. Plebes have a somewhat similar connotation presently, as they are first years who transition from civilian to military live at the US Naval Academy.

the Freshman Fifteen

(as in, how to avoid it)

Okay, so you're on your own for the first time. Mom's good ol' fashioned cooking is no longer waiting for you on the dinner table every night and you're faced with making decisions at every meal. What's an undergrad to do? The Dining Services Department at the University of Michigan put together a quiz for students to see how much they really know about nutrition and exercise. Turns out, the freshman fifteen is a result of...you guessed it: late night munchies, alcohol consumption, endless buffets at meal time with free refills of soda, and less activity than high school. For instance, if a person played 1 1/2 hours of field hockey twice a week in high school and replaced that activity with studying once they started college, and assuming there are no other changes to eating and activity, they would gain 14 ¼ pounds!

Frisbee

Ultimate Frisbee

For all those frisbee players out there, betcha didn't know there's an actual players association which culminates in a national tournament of ultimate frisbee for college teams! The College Championship Series hosts a series of tournaments which leads up to the College National Championships. Sponsored by the Ultimate Player's Association or UPA, the college division is composed of five regions throughout the country. Within each region there are lots of sections so any college may compete at their sectional tournament as long as they meet eligibility requirements. Women's teams like Stanford's "Superfly" and "Rumpus" or Northwestern's "Gung Ho" and men's teams like the University of Pennsylvania's "Void" or Tufts University's "E-men" take the competition seriously, by practicing throughout the week, in hopes of a championship season by winning the regionals.

Grades

Grade-free zone

In order to encourage students to pursue interests in a non-competitive environment, officials at New College in Florida decided not to issue grades. Yes, you read this right! No grades, but no problem?

Grease

Greasy Grease Trucks

Picture it. It's 2 a.m. and you're cramming for a Design & Analysis Statistical exam. Got a case of the munchies, you're craving something fried with cheese, and lots of it. If you're at Rutgers University in New Jersey, you head straight for College Ave., home of the Grease Trucks. That's right, vendor trucks cater to students selling all the essentials like cheese fries, burgers and gyros. Each truck has names such as the Sunrise Grease Truck, and students usually become friends with the vendors after visiting their trucks so often.

Greeks

1st Fraternity & 1st Sorority

Alpha Delta Phi, known as the first secret sisterhood, was founded at Wesleyan Female College in Macon, GA in 1851.

Kappa Alpha Society, the first fraternity was founded at Union College in Schenectady, NY in 1825. Soon after, Sigma Phi and Delta Phi were also founded at Union. These three fraternities were known as the Union Triad and the basis of all fraternities.

Gym

Let's get HYPER

Of course gymnasiums, as well as other buildings are named after benefactors but it's a little different at the University of Arkansas. Their gym, the Hyper Building, is an acronym for the House of Physical Education and Recreation.

Halloween

Dancing in the Streets

Call it the biggest bash of the year when students at Ohio University in Athens, Ohio prepare for their Halloween party. The OU administration closes off main street in town and students cover the town with Halloween decorations, decked out in orange and black. About 30,000 students gather for the festivities (that's double than the amount of students who actually attend OU!) They all party it up and dress in costumes in the streets of Athens.

The curse of Halloween

Every five years or so the haunts of Halloween circulate on several campuses close to one another, as experienced in 1986 and again in 1991. Students at Lafayette College, Lehigh University, Muhlenberg College, and Allentown College all heard of the prediction from Nostradamis, a psychic who's been dead for a few hundred years. Apparently, before he died, ol' Nostra declared that a mass murder would be committed at a college in PA on Halloween. The specifics were shady, but apparently it was to occur on a campus near railroad tracks or a river and in an 'h' or 'l'-shaped dorm, which could really apply to any college and any dorm. As hysteria escalated, rumors developed like hearing about a psychic who appeared on a major talk show and confirmed the Nostradamis prediction. Though no one could attest to this, it was always a friend of a friend who saw that show. Needless to say, no murder was committed on Halloween in '86 or '91 but it is certainly a rumor students won't forget!

Homecoming

A tradition is born

Apparently the tradition of homecoming in both high schools and college originated in 1911 by the University of Missouri's Athletic Director. That year the annual Missouri-Kansas game was scheduled to be played at a college campus for the first time. To cheer on the Tigers, the director pleaded with alumni to "come home" for the big game. About 9,000 alums went to the game, thereby combining the concept of football with "coming home", or Homecoming as we know it today.

Sink or Swim

Every year before Homecoming at the University of Miami in Florida, architecture students build a float, set it on fire and let it go on Lake Osceloa. Students gather and cheer to see if the boat will sink or not. According to legend, if the boat does not sink the Miami Hurricanes will win their football game.

Honor Codes

Thou Shall Not Cheat

At Hampden-Sydney College, students can expel each other for cheating, stealing or being dishonest. Students govern themselves with a student-run honor court assigned to decide punishment.

January break

Homework that's actually fun!

Attending jazz concerts in NYC is homework for Lafayette College students who register for the class over January break, known to Lafayette students as "interim". During this time when most students are at home relaxing or working a part-time job, some LC students take classes during the day with extensive real-life experiences outside the classroom. Classes are offered either in the US or abroad in various places such as the Bahamas, England, France, Germany, Scotland, Austria, Israel, Kenya and Tanzania.

Library

Accounting Pub Flub

Students at Princeton were creative in the 1800s when their library was converted to a student center with a popular pub. The prestigious school made a mistake at first because the building was still listed as a library in the accounting books after it became the student center. Enjoying their new pub, students ordered drinks and charged them to their student account. Conveniently the bills arrived at home and parents saw the charges listed as "Library Services". They must have thought their students were really studious that semester!

Majors

America's favorite weatherman

There are actually a few people out there who actually have a career based on what they studied in school. Just look at *The Today Show's* weatherman, Emmy winner and best-selling author Al Roker, alum of State University at Oswego, NY. While attending Oswego, Al landed a job as a weekend weatherman for a local tv station and hasn't looked back since!

Two all beef patties, special sauce, lettuce, cheese, pickles, onions on a sesame seed bun

Majoring in burgers is the goal for students who attend Hamburger University in Oakbrook, Illinois. Although you won't find undergrads at HU, you will find a team of restaurant managers who learn various aspects of the business. Known as McDonald's worldwide management training center, over 30 professors have taught the business basics to over 65,000 Mickey D's graduates. (Maybe they actually learn the recipe for the special sauce?)

Mascots

Go Ephs, Go!

Forget about the typical mascot like an eagle. At Williams College in Williamstown, Massachusetts, students and alumni alike root for the one and only Eph. That's right kids, they root for a purple cow named after the founder of the school, Ephraim Williams. The mascot (pronounced "eefs") represents a popular campus humor magazine, aptly named "the Purple Cow", that circulated in the early 1900s. In 1907, the student body voted in this purple cow as the official mascot.

Storm Watch

At St. John's University, home of the Red Storm, it's not unusual to for its mascots to fire up the crowd at the home basketball and football games. After all, their mascots are none other than "Thunder" and his sidekick, "Lightning"!

Meal Plan

Munch Money

At Georgetown University, one unique facet of the meal plan is called Munch Money. It's an account students can use on campus to pay for snacks, groceries, and local take-out.

Media

Satirical Read

Though its weekly student newspaper is called *The Campus* at Middlebury College, its biannual publication satires the campus gets the laughs going. Known as *The Crampus*, this humorous publication spoofs the Middlebury community and nation at large. In one of its spring editions it showed Middlebury clones, which showed several guys looking exactly alike, all wearing the same shirt, jeans and yes, the ubiquitous baseball cap!

Campus TV

At SCBN, Stanford Cardinal Broadcasting Network, this campus station not only reports on local campus events, its extensive programming is enough to rival that of a major network! There's a cooking show with culinary tips and laughs, a sketch comedy show, a variety show, political show, movies and even a drama which is set in a fictitious east coast college town.

Moving Out

The Ghost of Shelton Hall

As you move out of your dorm at the end of the year, you realize your room will soon belong to someone else, yet you can't help but think who lived there before you did. At Boston University in Shelton Hall's Suite 401, it's pretty clear it's former resident, American playwright Eugene O'Neill, lived there because he continues to spook occupants. Going back to the early 1980s, his spirit has been known to mysteriously appear in the way of an occasional flicker of the room's lights or a random knocking on the door.

In 1994, two resident advisors made sure Shelton Hall's windows were shut for the holiday break. They shut the window in suite 401 and thought they saw a figure run towards the same room even though the building was deserted. When they checked the room later, they found the locked window had been opened. Unsolved mystery!

Nicknames

The Fighting Irish

Ask anyone at Notre Dame and they'll tell you their athletic nickname is "The Fighting Irish". Though the origin of "The Fighting Irish" is still uncertain, one fabled tale says the press coined the term in the 1920s by describing the never-say-die fighting spirit and their Irish qualities of grit, determination and tenacity. The term actually began as an abusive statement towards the students at this private Catholic institution, however a Notre Dame alum popularized the term in the 1920s in his *New York Daily News* column.

Night before exams

Pres*ident's bed-time story*

The night before exams at William and Mary isn't a typical night of studying and stressing. Instead, in the fall semester there's an annual yule log ceremony in which students sing carols. Then they listen to the president, who is decked out in red pajamas, read a story called "'Twas the Night Before Exams".

Orientation

Huge Handshake

At Knox College in Illinois on the first day of school, every year students do The Pump Handle to meet every single student at Knox. Basically it's a two hour event where students line up and form a human chain so in the end you have shaken everyone's hand.

Parties

Mine, all mine!

Students at the University of Montana celebrate Forrester's Ball, an annual event whereby the gym is completely changed to resemble a mining town. Party revelers enter the ball through a mine shaft. Drinks and food are purchased in exchange for a kiss!

Phi Beta Kappa

Hipay EtaBay AppaKay (that's Greek Latin to you babe!)

Known as the first society with a greek letter name, Phi Beta Kappa is the nation's most prestigious honors undergraduate organization. It was founded in 1776 at the College of William and Mary and introduced characteristics of societies such as a secrecy oath, a badge, mottoes, codes of law, a handshake and an elaborate initiation.

Philanthropies

Pong-a-Thon

The Phi Delta Theta chapter at the University of Pennsylvania hosts an annual pong marathon to raise money for research of amyotrophic lateral sclerosis. Also known as Lou Gehrig's disease, ALS is a progressive neurodegenerative disease that attacks nerve cells in the brain and the spinal cord. Gehrig was diagnosed with ALS and retired from baseball at an early age. An incredible baseball player, he is known for playing in 2,130 consecutive baseball games, an amazing record that stood the test of time until it was recently broken. He's almost as well known for his "Today, I consider myself the luckiest guy on the face of the earth" speech at Yankee Stadium before retiring. He was a member of Phi Delt back in his collegiate days.

Juvenile Diabetes Foundation
Alpha Gamma Delta, the first sorority to establish an official philanthropy, founded the Alpha Gamma Delta camp for underprivileged children in 1919. Though the camp shut down in 1947, the focus on children remains a priority. Alpha Gams primarily donate their time, money, and effort to the Juvenile Diabetes Foundation. For instance, the Delta Sigma chapter of the University of Hawaii at Manoa participates in the annual JDF Walk to cure diabetes and takes part in other local community service such as making bookmarks to local school children to promote reading and by cooking and spending time with children at the Ronald McDonald House.

Pranks
The little pumpkin that could
Perched on top of a 173-foot tower, it was hard to believe a little orange pumpkin stayed intact for five months throughout the tumultuous winter at Cornell University in upstate New York. Even more astonishing was how the orange got placed there, several days before fall break in October 1997. Such is the tale of Cornell's Great Pumpkin, a modern day prank that gained national media coverage, a webpage with live video and a contest to determine scientific factors to see if it was a real pumpkin. Who knows how long it would have lasted if a crane didn't accidentally knock it down when construction occurred on campus in March '98!

To find out more about college pranks, like the 1982 Harvard-Yale football game in which MIT students launched a balloon from the 46-yard line so it inflated to full size with MIT written on it, read the one and only book on pranks, *If at All Possible, Involve a Cow, the Book of College Pranks* by Neil Steinberg.

Professors

The 4-1-1 on Frosh

Every year the staff at Beloit College in Beloit Wisconsin compiles a list to give the faculty a frame of reference for years in which the incoming freshmen were born. This mini-history lesson, such as indicating the freshmen were 1 year old the year a blockbuster movie was introduced, gives everyone a time frame for the incoming class. Not just for Beloit faculty, the list typically gets circulated via e-mail to tons of people.

Quad

Unspoken Tradition

When walking across the quad at Washington and Lee, students find themselves saying hello to people they don't even know. Actually, the unspoken tradition on campus is that you say hi to anyone you make eye contact with. That's one friendly school!

Radio stations

College Charts

Rock, country, college and rap are all styles of music any dj would be familiar with. With a genre all its own, the college music scene is where its at. In New Orleans, Tulane University's radio station, WTUL (91.5 on your local FM dial), brings alternative music to the city more famous for it's jazz and blues.

Registration

Time to call Caroline

At the University of North Carolina in Chapel Hill, the school's registration via a touch-tone phone is called "Caroline". Each graduating class is assigned a different weekend to call in and individual students are given a specific day to register.

Requirements

No Swimming past this point!

At Colgate, a 4 credit phys ed class is required in order to graduate and on top of that, students must pass a swim test! Apparently if you don't pass the swim test, rumor has it you must set up chairs at graduation.

Rivalries

Go team, go!

Ask most people what the most important game of the season is and they're bound to talk about an intense rivalry. The biggest of them all is the annual Lafayette-Lehigh game, which is college football's most played rivalry!

Schools	*Name of the Game*
Amherst v. Williams	The Biggest Little Game in America
Florida v. Florida State	The World's Largest Outdoor Cocktail Party
Jacksonville State v. Troy State	Battle for the Ol' School Bell
Mississippi State v. Ole Miss	The Egg Bowl
Oklahoma v. Oklahoma State	The Bedlam Game
Oregon vs. Oregon State	The Civil War
Pittsburgh v. West Virginia	Backyard Brawl
Texas v. Texas A&M	The Lone Star Showdown

Schools	*Prize*
Purdue v. Indiana	Old Oaken Bucket
Monmouth v. Knox	Bronze Turkey
Boston College v. Notre Dame	The Ireland Trophy
BYU v. Utah	The Beehive Boot
Carleton College v. St. Olaf	The Goat Trophy
Dickinson v. Franklin & Marshall	The Conestoga Wagon Trophy
Illinois v. Ohio State	A wooden turtle named "Illi-Buck"

Smells like School Spirit

Fans at University of Mississippi, a.k.a. Ole Miss, must have sore feet when their football games end. During the entire game fans are on their feet, cheering for Ole Miss, only to sit during half-time.

The Bonfire

Every year Aggies, students at Texas A& M University, build a 55 foot bonfire as an annual tradition prior to their game against the University of Texas. A few years ago the bonfire was fatal when several students died, leaving many to question the future of this dangerous tradition.

Road trip

It's a bird, it's a plane…it's a wienermobile?

Forget about a typical road trip visiting friends at another school. Traveling in the one and only Wienermobile is a road trip experience unlike any other! Once a year Oscar Mayer accepts applications from collegians throughout the country looking to spread "miles of smiles" in their hot dog shaped vehicle, aptly named the Wienermobile. After they've been selected, the group of 20 or so hotdoggers attends Hot Dog High to learn all about Oscar Mayer products and event planning which are essential to their year-long internship. After their training, they board the W-mobile to promote Oscar Mayer with fun stuff like appearances on the late night talk show circuit, MTV, charity and promotional events.

ROTC

In a class by itself

At schools such as the University of Massachusetts, it's clear that Army ROTC is a class unlike any other. ROTC students learn to fire an M16 rifle, navigate through a forest using a topographical map and a compass, and fly Army helicopter in training events. Better yet, the army provides uniforms and books. If students decide to become an officer in the Army, they must sign a contract by their junior year. Many students apply for 2, 3 and 4 year scholarships to help pay for school.

Scavenger Hunt

Hoopla on Michigan Ave.

If you see a U. of Chicago student completely covered in post-it notes, do not be alarmed, you are witnessing another great college tradition. Students at the University of Chicago can be found throughout the Windy City trying to find odds and ends for the annual scavenger hunt after midterms end. Students form teams to collect as many of the items on the list to earn cash prizes during the 24-hour event.

School Spirit

How Berkeley Can You Be?

This annual parade and festival at the University of California at Berkeley celebrates coming together and acting a little goofy, at least for a day. Featuring elaborately decorated floats, off-the wall music, strange music and people dressed as bumblebees, the parade is led by the Cal Marching Band. In recent years the parade winds through downtown and ends up at Martin Luther King Jr. Civic Center Park where people rejoice with food, drinks and more music.

Annual Boat Regatta

The University of Illinois at Champaign's Annual Boat Regatta is a huge event that draws crowds to cheer on its cardboard boats. That's right, the fastest cardboard boat with passengers to make it across the pool wins. Picture the most creative boats you can find such as the boat that shouts out sparks to begin the race in a cloud of smoke. The fun in the race is not so much who gets to the end first, but the spirit of the night. Awards given include the "titanic award" for the most spectacular sinking, an award for the most creative use of cardboard, the most outrageous design and the team with the most spirit. In a recent race, members of the American

Society of Civil Engineers wore bathrobes and towels on their heads and raced a yellow duck while others dressed as mermaids!

Security

Walksafe

Students at McGill University in Montreal can walk safely at night thanks to the student organization, Walksafe. This free escort service will walk you to and from any location in Montreal, 7 days a week!

Semester

Quarterly stuff

Although most schools have a fall and spring semester, some schools like UCLA or Stanford have three ten week periods of classes which means one thing: more midterms and finals than ever!

Snowball fights

Let it snow, let it snow, let it snow

At the University of Vermont, the first snowfall of the year signifies a long-lasting tradition on campus. Everyone drops what they're doing to pelt snowballs to their classmates in a huge campus-wide snowball fight on the main campus.

Spring break

Alternative Spring Break

Sure, you can go some place exotic with your friends for a week and get a really good tan. Or, you can go home, relax and veg out for a week. If you really want a unique experience you can volunteer during your break. For instance, for Alternative Spring Break at the University of Georgia, students volunteer their time to give back to the community such as going to North Carolina to build a house for a low-income family through Habitat for Humanity.

Statues

Targets for pranksters

Ah, the campus statue. Sitting pretty on the quad or wherever it may be located, statues have lots of stories surrounding them. John Harvard, a statue in Harvard Square, has been painted a Dartmouth green or a Yale blue. It has also worn a jumbo bronze MIT class ring on its finger and plaster casts on his head, neck and leg, all courtesy of MIT students.

At Cornell, students painted footprints of Ezra Cornell and Andrew D. White to imply that they hopped off their pedestals and later returned.

Painting statues is very common, as Tommy Trojan at USC has been painted so many times by UCLA rivals that it has been covered with canvas and plastic to avoid being painted again. Tommy's bronze sword has been stolen so many times, that the school replaced it with a wooden sword. Based on all the pranks, Tommy Trojan is now watched by a 24-hour video camera.

Traditions

Running of the Rodents

Every year, the week before finals at Spalding University in Kentucky, there's a show-down at noon in the campus parking lot. No it's not a huge fight between students or even a prayer group to get through finals. Instead, it's an actual rat race in which students sponsor rats in preparation for the Kentucky Derby. Rats race against one another for the winner's bowl and the grand prize: a garland of fruit loops worn by the fastest rat.

Hasty Pudding

The coveted Pudding Pot

Ask anyone at Harvard about the Hasty Pudding Theatricals and they'll tell you it's the oldest theatrical company in the country featuring a hilarious show starring male undergrads dressed in drag. Founded in the mid-1800s, originally members brought pudding to every meeting. Since all members were male, a guy played the role of a woman in the first performance. Today, students compete to write a humorous script for the annual production that's performed in Cambridge, MA, New York and Bermuda.

The show is only part of the fun, as each February the light-hearted theatrical company crowns two celebrities with the Man and Woman of the Year Awards for their lasting and significant contributions to entertainment. Both winners receive the coveted brass award trophy, the Pudding Pot, at their award ceremony featuring a roast of career highlights and not-so-memorable moments. The list of past honorees include Tom Cruise, Mel Gibson, Billy Crystal, Meg Ryan, Julia Roberts and Jamie Lee Curtis, among other celebs. For more info, check out www.hastypudding.org

Tuition

Barter system

Harvard University, the oldest institution in the US dating back to 1636, had an unusual tuition rate that wouldn't come close to the big bucks of today. Back then students, paid for their education with sugar, bacon, grain, or bushels of wheat.

Year

Battle of the Classes

It won't be a big deal when you have friends who are upperclassmen, though it wasn't always this nonchalant. Way back in the olden days (circa 1900s), there used to be huge rivalries between classes. Freshmen and sophomores, especially, used to hold tons of competitions such as a scrap. Scraps used to involve all freshmen and sophomores in a contest to push a giant ball to one end of a field. For instance, at Penn State freshmen had to sneak a barrel of cider on campus and deliver it to juniors. It was the sophomores job to spoil it by capturing the barrel before the frosh delivered it to the juniors.

At Hope College, years ago the freshman/sophomore battle was: a "cane rush" in which frosh and sophs competed to get the most hands from their class on the cane. A present-day rivalry currently exists at Hope College. Known as "the Pull", freshmen and sophs compete in a giant tug of war that's been a tradition at Hope since 1897! Basically there are two teams of 18 people pulling on a 600-foot, 1200-lb rope. Yikes!

Memories in the Making

You're hip. You're happening. You have the slang down to a science, you've digested the inside scoop on traditions, tales, and pranks, you're ready to rock and roll! Use this section as your pocket memory guide to keep track of the special (and silly) moments of your own college experience.

Overall thoughts

First memories walking on campus my very first day as a freshman

First impressions of my roommate

First true friend

The one thing I love most about being in college

I really didn't need to bring…

But I should have brought

The one thing I miss most about being away from home

Over fall break, the first thing I noticed that's different about being at home (i.e., a major highway constructed behind my house)

Best lesson learned outside of class

Best lesson learned inside of class

Things I want to do before I graduate

When I grow up I want to be...

Academics

This is the hardest class ever, I don't know what I was thinking when I registered for...

This class was the biggest blow off, I could skip all my classes and still ace the exam

Best excuse for an assignment extension

Number of times I've overslept and missed my 8 a.m. classes this semester

Coolest professor (you know, the one who lets you call him/her by his first name and is like a real person)

Worst professor and why

Number of hours spent in the library per week

Number of hours spent socializing in the library per week

This class is mostly likely to be held outside when the weather's nice

This class is so popular, even if I get on the waitlist I still won't get in

Number of all-nighters pulled this semester

Worst computer saga story (i.e., corrupt file after pulling an all-nighter)

Most incomprehensible, torturous assignment (i.e., reading *Dante's Inferno*)

Proudest assignment (I've worked so hard on this, I totally deserve an A)

Places I would consider studying abroad

Potential majors

Campus Life

My favorite building on campus

My least favorite building

The best place to go sledding or mudsliding

Best campus-wide tradition or annual event

Event with the best display of school spirit

Worst laundry mishap

Longest span of time I've gone without doing laundry

Dorm with the smallest closets

Dorm with the biggest closets

Dorm with best cable reception

Dorm with slowest internet connection

This dorm has the best location on campus…

But this dorm has the worst!

This is the party dorm

Next year I want to live with

In this dorm

Potential scary roommate—I would absolutely not want to live with this person

Most generic poster seen in practically everyone's room

Number of times this semester our fire extinguisher was stolen on our floor

This friend's dorm room is the place where all of my friends hang out

Number of times my roommate kicked me out of my room to entertain an overnight guest

Number of times I kicked out my roommate

Number of times I've lost my keys or id per week

Every time I lose them, I usually find them here:

Clubs/organizations I belong to

Most popular community service activity on campus

Number of times I've gone to the health center and was given aspirin and sent home

Finances

Average cost of books per semester

Average cost to do a load of laundry

Most money taken out of ATM machine at one time

Number of t-shirts bought from people selling them door-to-door

Funniest t-shirt slogan

Most expensive book bought in the bookstore

By selling my books at the end of the semester, I made this much money

Food

Best place to get coffee at 2 a.m.

Best Chinese food take-out

This meal in the cafeteria was so disgusting…

But this one was actually pretty good

Favorite fraternity kitchen to raid

Number of pounds I gained my first semester

Favorite food to munch on while studying

Favorite caffeinated beverage

The absolute best care package I ever got was sent by

Contents of my refrigerator right now

Social Life

Best place for face time on campus

This person has the best picture in the face book

Of course, face book is the polite term. At my school it's really called the ________ book.

Biggest scammer

Biggest flirt

Biggest BMOC or hottie

List of PFDs

Funniest moment ever, I laughed so hard I couldn't breathe when

Most embarrassing moment, I turned bright red when

Most stressful moment ever

Best prank pulled, this was a classic

Number of friends who got pinned

Number of friends who were pinned and later broke up

I had so much fun at this party…

But this bash was so boring, I couldn't wait to leave

Favorite theme party

If I go Greek, here are the top three houses I want to join

After rushing, this is the house I actually joined

Funniest or most outrageous nickname of a friend

My nickname is

Possible spring break destinations

Possible road trip destinations

Most random place I've hooked up on campus

The latest time in the morning I've done the walk of shame

Number of my strides of pride/walks of shame this semester

Latest time I came home from a party (for example, 6 a.m.)

Worst beer goggle ever. What was I thinking when I hooked up with…

Favorite Halloween costume (either my own or a friend's costume)

Worst formal date, going with this person was a disaster, I never want to see them again

Best formal date, this person was so much fun to be with

Best song to dance to

My parents would freak out if they only knew I…

Sign of the Times

Buzzwords/catch phrases my friends and I say all the time

Hottest songs on the charts

Favorite video

Favorite movie

This is the one primetime tv show that I'd drop everything to watch

Favorite website, this one is definitely bookmarked

Favorite celebrity (male)

Favorite celebrity (female)

Favorite professional athlete

Internet Fun

Here are some anonymous stories taken straight from the internet.

You know you're a college student if...

You live in a house with three couches, none of which match.
You consider Mac and Cheese a balanced meal.
You have ever written a check for 45 cents.
You have a fine collection of domestic beer bottles.
You have ever seen two consecutive sunrises without sleeping.
Your glass set is composed of McDonald's Extra Value Meal Plastic Cups.
Your underwear supply dictates the time between laundry loads.
You can not remember when you last washed your car.
You can pack your worldly possessions into the back of a pick-up.
You have ever had to justify yourself for buying Natural Light.
You average less than 3 hours of sleep a night.
Your trash is overflowing and your bank account isn't.
You go to Wal-Mart more than 3 times a week.
You eat in the cafeteria because it's "free" even though it sucks
You are personally keeping the local pizza place from bankruptcy
You wake up ten minutes before class
Your breakfast consists of a diet coke on the way to class.
Your social life consists of a date with the library.
Your idea of "doing your hair" is putting on a baseball cap.
It takes a shovel to find the floor of your room.
You carry less than a dollar on you at all times because that's all you have.

Your midnight snack is microwave popcorn
You celebrate when you find a quarter
You have built up a tolerance for certain beverages (hee hee)
You get more sleep in class than in your room
You can sleep through your roommate's blaring stereo.
You live in an area that is smaller than most mobile homes.
You get more e-mail than mail.

Freshmen vs. Seniors

Freshman: Is never in bed past noon.
Senior: Is never out of bed before noon.

Freshman: Reads the syllabus to find out what classes he can cut.
Senior: Reads the syllabus to find out what classes he needs to attend.

Freshman: Brings a can of soda into a lecture hall.
Senior: Brings a jumbo hoagie and six-pack of Mountain Dew into a recitation class.

Freshman: Calls the teacher "Professor".
Senior: Calls the professor "Bob".

Freshman: Would walk ten miles to get to class.
Senior: Drives to class if it's more than three blocks away.

Freshman: Memorizes the course material to get a good grade.
Senior: Memorizes the professor's habits to get a good grade.

Freshman: Knows a bookfull of useless trivia about the university.
Senior: Knows where the next class is. Usually.

Freshman: Shows up at a morning exam clean, perky, and fed.
Senior: Shows up at a morning exam in sweats with a baseball cap on and a box of pop tarts in hand.

Freshman: Lines up for an hour to buy textbooks in the first week.
Senior: Starts to think about buying textbooks in October...maybe.

Freshman: Looks forward to first classes of the year.
Senior: Looks forward to first beer bash of the year.

Freshman: Is proud of getting A on Calculus midterm
Senior: Is proud of not *quite* failing Complex Analysis midterm

Freshman: Calls his girlfriend back home every other night
Senior: Calls Domino's every other night

Freshman: Conscientiously completes all homework, including optional questions
Senior: Offers to "tutor" conscientious frosh of opposite sex

Freshman: Goes on grocery shopping trip with Mom before moving onto campus
Senior: Has a beer with Mom before moving into apartment

Freshman: Is excited about the world of possibilities that await, the unlimited vista of educational opportunities, the chance to expand one's horizons and really make a contribution to society
Senior: Is excited about new dryers in laundry room

Freshman: Takes meticulous four-color notes in class
Senior: Occasionally stays awake for all of class

A Letter Home

Dear Dad,

$chool i$ really great. I am making lot$ of friend$ and $tudying very hard. With all my $tuff, I $imply can't think of anything I need, $o if you would like, you can ju$t send me a card, a$ I would love to hear from you.

Love,
Your $on

Dear Son,

I kNOw that astroNOmy, ecoNOmics, and oceaNOgraphy, are eNOugh to keep even an hoNOr student busy. Do NOt forget that the pursuit of knowledge is a NOble task, and you can never study eNOugh.

Love,
Dad

College habits you can bring home

Try to use your dorm key to unlock your bedroom door
Have your mom scan your ID card for meals
Look for a tray to carry your dinner to the table with
Walk two blocks to go to dinner
Forget to dial the first three digits of your friend's phone number
Walk to the post office to get your mail
Yell "Heads Up" when you flush the toilet
Jump out of the shower just in case someone does flush
Take all your shower items to and from your room
Get dressed in the dark
Go nuts looking for the quarter slots in the washing machine
Make junk food runs at midnight
Make popcorn just because you miss the smell
Order pizza every night
Have one of your friends spend the night because you can't sleep in a room by yourself
Move another bed, dresser, and desk into your room because there is too much extra space
Hang pictures of your college friends on the wall so you don't miss them
Walk around the neighborhood looking for a computer lab (e-mail withdrawal)
Fight your mother for quarters for the imaginary snack machine and pay phone in the house.

The Night Before Finals

'Twas the night before finals and all through the college,
The students were praying for last minute knowledge.
Most were quite sleepy, but none touched their beds,
While visions of essays danced in their heads.

Out in the taverns, a few were still drinking,
And hoping that liquor would loosen up their thinking.
In my own room I had been packing,
And dreading exams I soon would be facing.

My roommate was speechless, his nose in his books,
And my comments to him drew unfriendly looks.
I drained all the coffee and brewed a new pot,
No longer caring that my nerves were shot.

I stared at my notes, but my thoughts were muddy,
My eyes were ablur, I just couldn't study.
"Some pizza might help," I said with a shiver,
But each place I called refused to deliver.

I'd nearly concluded that life was too cruel,
With futures depending on grades made in school.

When all of a sudden our doors opened wide,
And Patron Saint Put It Off in ambled inside.
His spirit was careless, his manner was mellow,
All of a sudden he started to bellow.

"On Cliffs Notes, on crib notes on last year's exams,

On Wingit and Slingit and last-minute crams."
His message delivered, he vanished from sight
But we heard him laughing outside in the night.

Your professors have pegged you so just do your best,
Happy Finals to all and to all a good test.

Before I came to college I wish I had known…

That it didn't matter how late I scheduled my first class I'd sleep right through it
That I would change so much and barely realize it
That you can love a lot of people in a lot of different ways
That college kids throw airplanes too
That if you wear polyester everyone will ask you why you're so dressed up
That every clock on campus shows a different time
That if you were smart in high school—so what?
That I would go to a party the night before a final
That chem labs require more time than all my other classes put together
That you can know everything and fail a test
That you can know nothing and ace a test
That I could get used to almost anything I found out about my roommate
That home is a great place to visit
That most of my education would be obtained outside my classes
That friendship is more than getting drunk together
That I would be one of those people my parents warned me about
That free food served at 10:00 is gone by 9:50
That Sunday is a figment of the world's imagination
That psychology is really biology, biology is really chemistry, chemistry is really physics and physics is really math
That my parents would become so much smarter in the past few years
That it's possible to be alone even when you're surrounded by friends
That friends are what makes this place worthwhile!
Don't be dismayed at goodbyes
A farewell is necessary before we can meet again, and meeting again, after moments or a lifetime, is certain for those who are friends.

AFTERWORD

You are embarking on the adventure of a lifetime. Don't be surprised if, by the end of your stint as a college student you have a nickname, wear your pajamas to class, go to a party after midnight, take tons of naps, live on caffeine, eat cereal for dinner, learn campus songs or Greek chants, have a Saturday final, pull at least one all-nighter, gain a new vocab ("The prof said she'll give us our grades right before break"), play at least one game of pong, and miss your friends over the long summers. You'll change without realizing it and learn to love every minute, even the studying (yes, the studying).

Work hard. Play hard. And have an amazing time!

INDEX

Index of Schools

About the Author

Vicki Salemi is a global mobility manager at a Big Five accounting firm but deep down she's a college kid at heart. Salemi graduated from Lafayette College and also studied abroad at McGill University in Montreal. In the little spare time that she has, Salemi volunteers for her alma mater and writes for *College Bound Magazine* and *Go-Girl.com.*

Printed in the United States
20529LVS00005B/367-369